A PRIMER FOR ICD-10-CM USERS

A
PRIMER FOR
ICD-10-CM
USERS

PSYCHOLOGICAL AND BEHAVIORAL CONDITIONS

CAROL D. GOODHEART

American Psychological Association · Washington, DC

Published by
American Psychological Association
750 First Street, NE
Washington, DC 20002
www.apa.org

To order
APA Order Department
P.O. Box 92984
Washington, DC 20090-2984
Tel: (800) 374-2721; Direct: (202) 336-5510
Fax: (202) 336-5502; TDD/TTY: (202) 336-6123
Online: www.apa.org/pubs/books
E-mail: order@apa.org

In the U.K., Europe, Africa, and the Middle East, copies may be ordered from
American Psychological Association
3 Henrietta Street
Covent Garden, London
WC2E 8LU England

Typeset in Stone Serif by Circle Graphics, Inc., Columbia, MD

Printer: United Book Press, Baltimore, MD
Cover Designer: Mercury Publishing Services, Rockville, MD

The opinions and statements published are the responsibility of the authors, and such
opinions and statements do not necessarily represent the policies of the American
Psychological Association.

Library of Congress Cataloging-in-Publication Data
Goodheart, Carol D., author.
  A primer for ICD-10-CM users : psychological and behavioral conditions / Carol D.
Goodheart. — First edition.
      p. ; cm.
  Includes bibliographical references and index.
  ISBN-13: 978-1-4338-1709-0
  ISBN-10: 1-4338-1709-8
  I. American Psychological Association, issuing body. II. Title.
  [DNLM: 1. International statistical classification of diseases and related health
problems. 10th revision. Clinical modification. 2. International statistical
classification of diseases and related health problems. 11th revision 3. Mental
Disorders—classification. 4. Forms and Records Control—methods. 5. International
Classification of Diseases. 6. Medical Records. WM 15]
  RC455.2.C4
  616.89001'2--dc23
                                        2013045447

British Library Cataloguing-in-Publication Data
A CIP record is available from the British Library.

Printed in the United States of America
First Edition

http://dx.doi.org/10.1037/14379-000

Contents

Acknowledgments

I thank the many colleagues who have supported the quest for meaningful diagnoses, psychological services, and outcomes over the years. I appreciate the assistance of those named here who have offered information and suggestions for this primer, and who believe that it is well worth trying to improve the clinical utility of the tools we use every day for psychotherapy to make a difference in our patients' lives. My gratitude goes especially to Geoffrey Reed for his vision and for more than a decade of collaboration on always interesting projects; to Lynn Bufka for her generous feedback and contributions to my thinking; and to Donna Pickett, Dorothy Cantor, Katherine Nordal, Jamie Walkup, Louise Douce, Michael C. Roberts, Spencer Evans, Bonnie Markham, the American Psychological Association (APA) Board of Professional Affairs, the APA Publisher Gary VandenBos, Senior Director for APA Books Julia Frank-McNeil, Acquisitions Editor Susan Reynolds, and the ICD series Consultant Editor Claude Conyers. Kudos to the APA and the APA Practice Organization for their early recognition of the importance of the ICD revision process and its clinical implications for public health. My family has once again tolerated long work hours and lovingly offered encouragement—thank you Leigh, Rich, Kate and Emily; Pam, Bridget, Michael and Brenna; and Becca and Bob.

A
PRIMER FOR
ICD-10-CM
USERS

CHAPTER 1

Introduction

The purpose of this primer is twofold. The first aim is to give psychologists and other mental health professionals the information necessary to use the World Health Organization's 10th edition of the *International Classification of Diseases* (ICD–10; 1992a), with clinical modifications for the United States (ICD–10–CM; Centers for Disease Control and Prevention, 2014). The second and equally important goal is to pave the way for the successful adoption and use of ICD–11. Under the terms of the 1996 U.S. Health Insurance Portability and Accountability Act, adherence to ICD diagnostic coding guidelines is required in all health care settings. An updated system that makes diagnosis more clinically useful and accurate is long overdue. This need is addressed to a modest extent by ICD–10–CM, which will be followed closely by ICD–11, with its greatly enhanced clinical utility features. During this transition period, mental and behavioral health clinicians in the United States have a meaningful opportunity to embrace the ICD system, as their colleagues have done in other parts of the world.

The intent of this primer is to prepare clinicians to adapt comfortably to the coming major revisions in the ICD system that will offer systemic changes for the better, starting with ICD–10–CM, which will be implemented on October 1, 2014. Many practitioners who provide mental and behavioral health services actually use only about eight different codes, making the task of understanding which codes to use and how to select them much easier.

This primer provides the essentials: an overview of the ICD system and its evolutionary strides, an understanding of ICD–10–CM, an explanation of the differences from ICD–9–CM (the official version used in the United States until October 2014; National Center for Health Statistics and Centers for Medicare and Medicaid Services, 1979), the strengths and limitations of classifications, the elements involved in making a diagnosis versus simply selecting a diagnostic code, and an introduction to ICD–11 (which is under development, with expected release in 2015). If readers familiarize themselves now with ICD–10–CM, the transition to ICD–11, with its many positive revisions backed by solid field trials, will be readily understood and well worth the effort. ICD–11 is expected to be a clear improvement over all previous revisions.

Before attending to the practical details of the ICD system, most practitioners and training faculty are likely to be interested in grasping the big picture: why we should care about the ICD and how the current updating process, resulting first in ICD–10–CM and then ICD–11, is highly relevant to our clinical practices. After all, the ICD, not the *Diagnostic and Statistical Manual of Mental Disorders* (DSM), is the official system used across all health settings in the United States. The process of conversion to using ICD–10–CM and then ICD–11 is already in motion, with a compelling reason for psychologists' involvement. Clinicians have a choice and a voice in deciding which diagnostic classification system they will find most useful for guiding mental and behavioral health practice in the future. Many clinicians have not realized this over the years and thought they were using, and were required to use, the DSM classification system. Yet, 95% of the world's health professionals (including physicians, nurses, and psychologists) already use ICD–10. Implementation of ICD–10–CM and ICD–11 are major steps toward psychology's globalization.

Although we often talk about globalization as if it were to occur in the future, many psychologists in the United States are already treating patients who have come to the United States from different countries around the world. It is important to use a diagnostic classification system that is based on international collaboration and can be adapted across a wide range of cultures.

Changes in demographics and infrastructure have changed how psychology views itself (Bullock, 2012): A generation ago, the United States had more psychologists than any other country, the language of psychology was predominately English, and most psychologists were academics. Now, both Latin America and Europe have more psychologists than the United States; Asia, Africa, and the Caribbean have developed their own local contexts for psychology; and psychology's growth around the world has been in the applied areas that are relevant to localized practical needs. Concurrently, the infrastructure of psychology education has changed, with the development of faculty and advanced psychology programs in most regions of the world. All of these changes have stimulated interest in identifying fundamental psychological constructs that also reflect local perspectives. The increased focus on understanding and balancing the universal and the particular to explain human behavior and function has propelled psychology forward. In this global context, the ICD facilitates communication among health care professionals and between health care professionals and patients. It is able to do so because of its internationally derived foundation that allows for clinical modifications to fit each country's unique needs.

The Centers for Medicare and Medicaid Services has recommended that organizations plan for the implementation of ICD–10–CM and develop education and training tools (2012b). This primer represents an attempt by the American Psychological Association and the American Psychological Association Practice Organization to put the necessary information into the hands of psychologists and other interested mental and behavioral health professionals.

The rollout of ICD–10–CM in 2014, followed by the gradual integration of ICD–11 after it is adopted by the World Health Organization's World Health Assembly in 2015, is expected to result in increased clinical accuracy, ease of use of the ICD system, and a newly designed architecture in ICD–11 that is based on how experienced practitioners naturally sort and group the information they learn from patients' clinical presentations. ICD–11 will be a substantial improvement for practitioners because it reflects their perspectives and priorities, and it offers a cultural framework as an essential element in the design. The diagnoses that clinicians make have a profound impact on the treatments offered and the clinical case management they choose. Diagnoses are also used to define governmental responsibilities for providing health services, including psychological services. For clinicians, the purpose of using any diagnostic classification system is to organize clinical information into a coherent understanding of the patient's health status (including a diagnosis or multiple diagnoses as well as knowledge of the resources available to the patient—internal and external). Once the patient's symptoms, function, presentation, schemas, resources, and cultural and personal contexts are organized into an appropriate diagnosis, the clinician can then develop a treatment plan to meet the patient's goals. The selection of a diagnosis allows treating clinicians to communicate in a common language with other health professionals and with patients and their families.

The goal for practitioners is the best care possible. Researchers, epidemiologists, public health officials, health systems, and coding specialists have their own interests and need for a uniform and accurate diagnostic classification system (e.g., for the creation of sound government policies to advance public health). But the system has to function first for the clinicians who are working in the service of patient care. The treating professionals are the first link in the chain of reporting on health status, in which mental and behavioral health form an integral part. The clinicians provide important information that is later aggregated in increasingly sophisticated data sets to report on matters vital to healthy and productive lives globally.

The World Health Organization considers the clinical utility of the ICD to be a global public health concern, for good reasons (Reed, 2010): For people in developed nations, 35.5% to 50% of those with serious mental disorders received no treatment in the past year, while in developing countries, 76.3% to 85.4% did not receive treatment over the same period (World Health Organization World Mental Health Survey Consortium, 2004). This highlights the serious treatment gap that ranges from 32% to 78% and varies by disorder and country resources (Kohn, Saxena, Levav, & Saraceno, 2004). There are many people who need the services of well-trained mental and behavioral health professionals with a commitment to the life-long learning needed to stay up to date. Clinicians need tools that evolve with new knowledge and that are kept current to enhance diagnostic skills and serve our communities well.

Clinicians can remain active and enhance diagnostic usefulness by anticipating and learning about ICD–10–CM first and then about ICD–11, which will follow shortly afterward. In the longer term, the advantages of ICD–11 over ICD–10 and ICD–10–CM will become more obvious. The ICD–11 development focus on a new architecture to enhance clinical utility in field settings, where patients are seen and treated, will benefit patients, psychologists and other mental health professionals, primary care physicians, health systems, researchers, and most of all, public health.

CHAPTER 2

Overview of the ICD

The World Health Organization (WHO), an agency of the United Nations (UN), is responsible for the development and updating of the *International Classification of Diseases* (ICD; WHO, 1992a). In fact, health classifications are a core constitutional obligation for the WHO.

History

The UN was formed in 1945, a time of international reverberations and geographic boundary changes in the aftermath of World War II. The UN founded WHO because it foresaw the need for specialized agencies and organizations to handle global matters in areas such as health, labor, and trade. WHO headquarters were established in Geneva, Switzerland, but the link between global health and global peace was strongly defined by placing a WHO office in the UN headquarters in New York too.

Today there are more than 7,000 WHO public health experts and employees trained to manage administrative, financial, and information systems—approximately 1,800 staff members in Geneva and the remainder in six regional offices and 150 individual country and area offices around the world (WHO, 2013a). The regional offices function as a repository of resources, and they offer technical support to governments and provide information to health professionals. Moreover, the ICD is a free and open resource, available on the Internet (http://www.who.int/classifications/icd/en/).

Iwo Moriyama, Ruth Loy, and Alistair H.T. Robb-Smith wrote a *History of the Statistical Classification of Diseases and Causes of Death*, which was edited and updated by Rosenberg and Hovert in 2011. It is a revealing account of special note because of the personal involvement of the authors. Moriyama and Robb-Smith began their involvement in preparations for the ICD–6 revision (WHO, 1948) and worked on each succeeding revision though ICD–9 (WHO, 1979). Loy aided the WHO secretariat with the revision process for ICD–8 (WHO, 1965) through ICD–10 (WHO, 1992a). The information that follows on the development of the ICD is attributable, with appreciation, to the work of Moriyama, Loy, and Robb-Smith (2011), with two exceptions separately cited.

In early medical history, nomenclatures were used. These were simple lists of names for diseases that were typically arranged in alphabetical order. Nomenclatures of diseases later became classification systems when they were organized in more meaningful ways, according to topography (location in the body) and later according to etiology (cause of the disease).

The stimulus for the development of the ICD was a serendipitous one. In 1851, at the Great Exhibition at the Crystal Palace in London, visiting statisticians saw the products of many nations on display, and they became interested in the idea of statistically comparing quantity, quality, and other characteristics of industrial goods. This led to the First International Statistical Conference in 1853 in Brussels, where cause of death was one of the topics considered for comparison across nations. Thereafter, the congress met every other year until 1878. It was succeeded by the International Statistical Institute (ISI), whose biennial meetings continue today.

In 1893, still long before the establishment of the UN and WHO, the ISI adopted the first edition of an international classification system, the *International List of Causes of Death*. It was a great success in its day. Three men are recognized as the founders: William Farr, Marc d'Espine, and Jacques Bertillon. The basis for the adopted list was developed originally in 1891 by Jacques Bertillon in France, who was also the leader for several decennial revisions. By 1899, Bertillon's "Causes of Death" system for ISI had been published in four languages and adopted in the United States, Mexico, Canada, and much of South America. One year earlier, the American Public Health Association passed a resolution recommending revision of the classification every 10 years, entrusting the revision to an international committee. The United States has been committed to the ICD from its earliest phases.

The *International List of Causes of Death* included diseases that were defined at the time and were deemed important to include because of their frequent occurrence or transmission to others. There was no category of mental disorders, although there was a category for diseases of the nervous system and sense organs. The international group established a 10-year revision cycle to stay abreast of progress in medicine. In each decade more countries began to adopt the list. The first revision, ICD–1, was made by the ISI in 1900 and was in use from 1900 to 1906. It kept the same basic structure as the original except that the first category, General Diseases, was divided into two categories, Epidemic Diseases and Other General Diseases. The translation of the second version, released by the U.S. Department of Commerce and Labor in 1909 (in use 1910–1920), was renamed the *International Classification of Causes of Sickness and Death* and added a section on causes of stillbirths. In the third version, which was delayed by World War I until 1920 (in use 1921–1929), the ISI made additions to the list and created new classification rubrics. Jacques Bertillon, a major force since its inception, died after the third revision conference. An international commission, known as the *Mixed Commission*, was created with an equal number of representatives from the International Statistical Institute and the Health Organization of the League of Nations to develop the fourth version, adopted in 1929 (in use 1930–1938; WHO, n.d.). This version retained the categories of diseases according to anatomical site, but the Institute committee realized it was feasible to change this progressively to categories based on etiology, as knowledge of disease etiology grew. The etiology principle guided the later revisions. The fifth revision, drafted by the Mixed Commission and adopted in 1938 (in use 1939–1948), incorporated some changes but largely gave practical consideration to the issue of comparability between successive versions of the ICD. It became the model for future revisions when the 1938 conference committee recommended a comparability of deaths study by dual classification in 1940, using both the fourth and fifth versions as a bridge between the two versions.

The WHO constitution was ratified on April 7, 1948, a date now celebrated annually as World Health Day (Vijayan, 2007). WHO was entrusted with the ICD that same year. The First World Health Assembly (WHA) adopted ICD–6, titled the *International Statistical Classification of Diseases, Injuries, and Causes of Death*, on July 24, 1948. WHO published ICD–6 with many changes to the content and the range of applications. This version included morbidity for the first time, in addition to the long-standing classification of mortality statistics (WHO, 2013b). By then, ICD–6 contained 800 categories of disease. It also included the concept of tabulating the primary cause of death, and the classification system had a strengthened legal framework. Notably, a new main category was introduced in ICD–6: Mental, Psychoneurotic, and Personality Disorders.

After the major changes in ICD–6, the 1955 revision for ICD–7 (in use 1958–1967) had a limited number of changes, to give countries a chance to adopt the morbidity classification introduced in ICD–6. Also, for practical reasons, the WHO Committee on Health Statistics recommended that revision conferences be held in years ending in 5 and applied to mortality in years ending in 8, so that countries could gain experience in use of the revised classification before national census figures, typically collected in years ending in 0 or 1, were available.

Following that recommendation, ICD–8 was adopted in 1965 (in use 1968–1978). By then, the conference committee recognized that the ICD could be expanded to serve as a diagnostic cross-index for hospital histories. It was influenced by adaptations in Israel, Sweden, and the United States for diagnostic indexing of clinical records in hospitals. In a similar vein, a Spanish translation by WHO's regional organization, the Pan American Health Organization, facilitated hospital use in Latin American countries. Significant revisions were made in several sections, including mental disorders.

In 1975, ICD–9 was adopted (in use 1979–1994). It kept the same general arrangement as the previous version. Because international standardized terminology did not exist for mental disorders, this revision included narrative descriptions for these disorders. Descriptions in ICD–9 were similar to language in the Manual of the American Psychiatric Association at the time (American Psychiatric Association, 1968).

The current WHO version, ICD–10, was approved by the WHA in 1990 (in use from 1994 to the present). Since then, it has been cited in 20,000 scientific articles globally. But new knowledge continues to accumulate, and the need for better classification continues to grow. As a result, approval by the WHA of the next revision, ICD–11, is expected in 2015.

The ICD began more than a century ago as a cooperative statistical effort to improve public health. As the ICD has evolved, its use has expanded beyond statistical purposes to medical record indexing, automated coding software for mortality, and reimbursement for medical services, including psychological and behavioral health services. How could anyone have imagined at the outset that despite world wars, financial crises, epidemics, and the inevitable advancements in and corrections to scientific knowledge, an international alliance could succeed in advancing a standard of health information reporting of such distinctive influence? Many challenges that are associated with classification remain to be solved. Yet the international cooperation in the steady revision of the ICD system—now translated into 43 languages—has been remarkable, as has been its acceptance.

Present Day

Today, the ICD system is the clinical and research standard for the world, for both physical and mental disorders. It is the global standard in diagnostic classification for health reporting and clinical applications across all diseases, disorders, injuries, and related health problems. The United States is one of the 194 WHO member countries that have agreed by international treaty to use the ICD as the uniform coding mechanism for reporting mortality and morbidity and other health information. The WHO constitution was developed to conform to the UN charter, and each country that wishes to become a member must agree to adhere to the constitution's principles. Thus, the ICD global reporting framework facilitates WHO's ability to fulfill its mission to attain the highest possible level of health for people around the world. In seeking to fulfill the mission, WHO's work involves promoting global health standards, tracking epidemics, monitoring disease burden, identifying important targets for health care resources, encouraging public health accountability, and facilitating the use of electronic health record systems for uniform record keeping (Ritchie, 2013).

WHO understands the wide variety of conditions, cultures, and infrastructure capacities of its many member nations. On the basis of that understanding, WHO allows countries to make clinical modifications to the ICD to fit each nation's health system needs and still remain compliant with the global reporting standard. The United States is one of the countries that makes clinical modifications, hence the use of the terms *ICD–9–CM* and *ICD–10–CM*. It is likely that ICD–11, forthcoming in 2015, will contain modifications in the United States and will be named *ICD–11–CM*.

Because of WHO's health monitoring activities over a lengthy period of time, we have gained a great deal of important public health information relevant to the work done by psychologists and other mental health professionals. For example, we have learned that depression is the leading cause of disability globally and that this disease burden is 50% higher for females than males (WHO, 2008). Overall, mental and neurological disorders account for greater disease burden than any other category, with the exception of communicable diseases (WHO, 2008). The valuable data and reports that stem from monitoring activities make it easy to understand why WHO views the clinical utility of its classification systems as a global public health issue (Reed, 2010).

Many psychologists and other mental health professionals in the United States are not familiar with the ICD, and just as few are familiar with the WHO's (2001) *International Classification of Functioning, Disability, and Health* (ICF). The ICF, a companion to the ICD, is another valuable diagnostic tool that is discussed in Chapter 3 of this primer. Many know the ICD, if at all, only as a reimbursement tool used to assign diagnostic codes for billing purposes, as required by the Health Insurance Portability and Accountability Act (HIPAA). When the ICD–9–CM code set was initially adapted for the United States in 1979 by the National Center for Health Statistics (NCHS) and Centers for Medicare and Medicaid Services (CMS), it was used for research purposes and for reporting health statistics only. In 1983, it also began to be used for reporting on health care services for reimbursement purposes.

Mental health practitioners in the United States have been taught primarily to use the *Diagnostic and Statistical Manual of*

Mental Disorders, Fourth Edition (DSM–IV; American Psychiatric Association, 1994) and DSM–IV–TR (text revision; American Psychiatric Association, 2000). Gradually, practitioners will be trained to use ICD–10–CM and ICD–11 (Centers for Disease Control, 2013), as well as the DSM–5 (American Psychiatric Association, 2013a), and these practitioners will outnumber those who are only familiar with the DSM system. Practitioners are often unaware that DSM diagnostic codes are translated (or "cross-walked") into ICD codes for billing, reimbursement, and federal reporting. DSM–IV–TR (American Psychiatric Association, 2000) and DSM–5 include the ICD codes in an appendix, because ICD diagnostic codes are required by HIPAA standards.

The revision of the DSM has been the subject of significant controversy among professionals, scientists, and concerned members of the public. However, far fewer in the United States have realized that the ICD was also undergoing revision, despite WHO's transparent and scientific process. The revision is of significance to practitioners because increasingly, with wider direct use of ICD–10–CM and ICD–11, U.S. mental and behavioral health clinicians can be realigned with the global ICD classification system. We do not need to remain essentially isolated in the DSM system.

It makes matters confusing that the United States is on a different schedule for adopting the ICD revisions than WHO and most of the other nations of the world. The following global timetable shows the work that has been accomplished to update the ICD and accommodate the changes in health care information needs over time:

> ➢ 1975: ICD–9 was endorsed by WHA, which includes the ministers and officers of health from all of the WHO member countries.
> ➢ 1990: ICD–10 was endorsed by the WHA and has been in wide use by WHO member states since 1994 (except for the United States).
> ➢ 2005: The WHA directed WHO to begin a revision of ICD–10.
> ➢ 2014: Technical work on ICD–11 is scheduled for completion.
> ➢ 2015: WHA approval of ICD–11 is expected.

By contrast, in

> ➢ 2013: The United States still uses the ICD–9–CM system put into place in 1979.
> ➢ 2014: The United States will implement ICD–10–CM (20 years later than other countries and 1 year before the rest of the world ushers in ICD–11).

Why is there such a lag in the United States? A bit of history and explanation is in order.

The National Committee on Vital and Health Statistics (NCVHS), the public advisory body to the Secretary of the U.S. Department of Health and Human Services (USDHHS), recognized more than 20 years ago that ICD–9–CM was no longer adequate to keep pace with changes in health care knowledge. Hence the committee recommended a change to ICD–10 for reporting mortality and morbidity health data (NCVHS, 2000). The CMS recommended either making improvements to ICD–9–CM's flexibility or replacing it (Zeisset & Bowman, 2010). In 1994, the NCHS asked the Center for Health Policy Studies to evaluate ICD–10, assess whether it was significantly better than ICD–9–CM for morbidity reporting, recommend any needed improvements to ICD–10, and correct any identified problems. They concluded that ICD–10 was not significantly better for morbidity reporting but that a clinical modification of ICD–10 would be worth implementing (Pickett, 2012).

The United States reports mortality data (death certificates), using ICD–10 (and has done so since 1999), but it remained the only developed nation in 2013 not to use it for reporting morbidity (diagnoses). The United States has continued to report morbidity based on ICD–9–CM.

ICD–10–CM has undergone many reviews in preparation for the implementation launch date in 2014. NCHS posted ICD–10–CM draft tabular list and crosswalks for public comment on its website as early as 1997. They posted the prerelease version in 2002. The American Health Information Management Association and the American Hospital Association then pilot tested it in 2003.

The USDHHS considered waiting for ICD–11 instead of creating a clinical modification of ICD–10, but decided it was not feasible to delay further, because the WHA adoption date for ICD–11 was uncertain and additional codes were sorely needed. Some medical specialties had run out of codes. Also, there was no ability to code "laterality," such as a left eye or a right leg, when needed. The distinctions between the left and right sides of the body (laterality) are not applicable to most disorders treated by mental health professionals, but the ICD is used for all physical and mental disorders and therefore serves all health care professionals.

ICD–9–CM is so outdated that it simply can no longer support current needs for health information. In addition, ICD codes are central to health information technology systems, with the rapidly growing use of electronic health records. As one might imagine, resistance to change in many sectors that will be affected by a new code set has been a constant factor and seems to be one reason why the process has taken such a long time. USDHHS made its first ruling in 2008; the fourth and final ruling in 2012 established the implementation date of ICD–10–CM as October 1, 2014 (CMS, 2012c).

NCHS, a part of the Centers for Disease Control and Prevention in the USDHHS, has worked diligently to develop ICD–10–CM in three phases: (a) the development of a prototype, (b) the development of enhancements by NCHS, and (c) the development of additional enhancements on the basis of feedback from many professional association groups, such as those representing physicians and nurses. Psychology associations were not among the major acknowledged reviewer groups, although the American Psychological Association (APA) did offer comments and feedback during the review period.

As the process unfolds, there is a freeze in effect for any changes to ICD–10–CM until October 2015. However, professional organizations such as APA and the American Psychiatric Association, and others, may submit suggested changes through the NCHS public comment process during the freeze. Any suggestions that are approved will not be implemented until after the freeze ends. Updates to ICD–10–CM may begin to be incorporated after October 2015.

Readers interested in more background information on the ICD before delving into the practical usage information in Chapter 3 can find the WHO introduction (2013b; http://www.who.int/classifications/icd/en/) and refer to Moriyama et al.'s *History of the Statistical Classification of Diseases and Causes of Death* (2011).

CHAPTER 3

The ICD–10–CM

Before reading this chapter and the ones that follow, I suggest readers look through the Appendix for orientation. It may be helpful to select a frequently used diagnosis or diagnostic category and keep it in mind. In looking through the diagnoses, it becomes apparent that one does not have to know all the digits and the inclusions and exclusions that are explained in this chapter, because they are provided for each diagnosis in the code set as published.

The structure and diagnostic codes for mental and behavioral disorders in the 10th edition of the *International Classification of Diseases* with clinical modifications for the United States (ICD–10–CM; Centers for Disease Control and Prevention [CDC], 2014) are established in the ICD–10 framework (World Health Organization [WHO], 1992a). It is quite different from ICD–9 (WHO, 1979) and the *Diagnostic and Statistical Manual of Mental Disorders* (4th ed., text rev.; DSM–IV–TR; American Psychiatric Association, 2000), the frameworks with which mental and behavioral health clinicians in the United States are most familiar. ICD–10–CM replaces ICD–9–CM (CDC, 2011). As a result, clinicians will need to understand the new system and how to use it. However, because the same categories of disorders are retained, practitioners must learn only the rearrangement of disorder categories and the new alphanumeric codes that replace the numeric codes in the previous iteration.

Two Important Distinctions

It should be noted that ICD–10–CM contains diagnostic codes, not procedure codes. *Procedure codes* differ from diagnostic codes in that they are designed to communicate the services and procedures delivered to patients. Procedure codes include such services as psychotherapy and psychiatric initial evaluations. In January 2013, clinicians and health systems in the United States were required to implement the new procedure codes established by the Current Procedural Terminology (CPT) Editorial Panel of the American Medical Association. Unlike the procedure codes, the ICD diagnostic codes, established by the various revision steering groups of the World Health Organization, are intended for worldwide use. The forthcoming change to ICD–10–CM does not affect the CPT codes.

It is also important to note that ICD–10–CM codes are to be used for outpatient treatment. A variation, called the ICD Procedure Coding System (ICD–10–PCS; Centers for Medicare and Medicaid Services [CMS], 1998), is intended for inpatient settings. CMS is the agency responsible for maintaining the inpatient procedure code set in the United States. American hospitals, like those in the rest of the world, use trained coders for recording and billing, and they generally use the PCS version for both diagnostic and procedure coding. The PCS version is not relevant, of course, for psychologists who provide outpatient services.

Rationale for Adopting ICD–10–CM

ICD–9–CM is more than 30 years old and obsolete. It does not provide sufficient health data or accurately describe diagnoses. Fundamentally, it cannot keep pace with health care in the electronic communications and record-keeping era.

According to the National Center for Health Statistics (NCHS; Pickett, 2012), the new coding system facilitates the use of updated medical terminology and disease classification, as well as facilitating the comparison of mortality and morbidity data. Up until now, the United States has been using ICD–9–CM for morbidity and ICD–10 for mortality. NCHS experts predict that the new coding system will provide better data for such diverse uses as claims processing, payment systems development, patient care measurement, clinical decision making, public health monitoring, fraud identification, and research. This array of improvements represents quite a step forward for the U.S. health care system.

A significant benefit of the new ICD–10–CM code adoption is the improved fit with computerized coding technology and the increased use of electronic health records, at what many people hope will be lower health system costs. Health care costs are an ongoing concern, as U.S. government legislators, employers, and insurers in the private and public sectors seek sustainable high-quality care while trying to slow an unsustainable growth curve in health care costs. However, it remains to be seen whether electronic health records are more cost-efficient in the long run. Apart from issues of cost, the global use of the system will most certainly allow for better international comparisons of patient care quality and permit easier sharing of best health practices.

In practical terms, ICD–10–CM offers many more codes and covers a wider range of diagnostic scope and content. It increases the available level of clinical detail and revises earlier, outdated descriptors of diseases and disorders. Perhaps most significantly, it is much more flexible and allows space in the system for additional codes. New codes are necessary as scientific knowledge inevitably advances and there is pressure to more accurately capture health conditions with accurate diagnoses.

Differences Between ICD–9–CM and ICD–10–CM Structures

There are substantially more codes available for use in the new ICD–10–CM structure, as is apparent in the side-by-side comparison shown in Table 3.1. This is almost a five-fold leap in the number of codes, which may seem overwhelming at first. However, there are two mitigating factors. First, for the most part, psychologists do not use the entire ICD but only the chapter on mental, behavioral, and neurodevelopmental disorders. Second, the hierarchical decimal coding structure is easy to understand.

ICD–10–CM is the first revision that includes letters, in addition to numbers, for the codes. All of the mental and behavioral disorder codes begin with the letter *F*. Although there is room for up to seven characters, most of the diagnostic categories in mental and behavioral disorders have four or five characters, with additional characters as needed in a number of instances for

TABLE 3.1
Differences Between ICD–9–CM and ICD–10–CM Structures

ICD–9–CM	ICD–10–CM
• 14,025 codes • 3–5 characters • First character is a number or letter • Characters 2–5 are numbers • Always at least 3 characters • Decimal is used after 3 characters	• 68,069 codes • 3–7 characters • First character is a letter • Second character is a number • Characters 3–7 are letter or number • Decimal is used after 3 characters • Use of dummy placeholder *x* • Letters are not case-sensitive

greater specificity. This is especially evident in the substance use categories, which have been greatly expanded. Codes with identical first three alpha (letter) and numeric (number) characters share common traits and belong to the same category. For example, the first three characters for alcohol related disorders are F10. Each number after the first three characters adds to the specificity (e.g., Alcohol dependence, uncomplicated, is F10.20, and Alcohol dependence with withdrawal is F10.23). More detail is available as needed with additional numbers.

Organization Overview

Anyone may download a copy of ICD–10–CM from the CDC website (http://www.cdc.gov/nchs/icd/icd10cm.htm#icd2014). Under the "2014 release of ICD–10–CM" heading, select the "ICD–10–CM List of codes and Descriptions (updated 7/3/2013)" link and then select the "ICD10CM_FY2014_FULL_PDF. zip" link from the FTP directory. There are 21 chapters in the list of diseases and injuries included in ICD–10–CM (ICD10CM_FY2014_Full_PDF_Tabular).

Chapter 5, "Mental, Behavioral, and Neurodevelopmental Disorders," may be found on pages 193–234 of the document and in the Appendix of this primer. The chapter has been revised structurally in substantial ways. For instance, codes within different diagnostic category sections are rearranged, some category and subcategory titles are changed, codes for substance use are increased, and intellectual disability codes have sequencing changes. The chapter is organized into diagnostic categories as follows:

> ➤ F01–F09 Mental disorders due to known physiological conditions
> ➤ F10–F19 Mental and behavioral disorders due to psycho-active substance use
> ➤ F20–F29 Schizophrenia, schizotypal, delusional, and other non-mood psychotic disorders
> ➤ F30–F39 Mood [affective] disorders
> ➤ F40–F48 Anxiety, dissociative, stress-related, somatoform and other nonpsychotic mental disorders
> ➤ F50–F59 Behavioral syndromes associated with physio-logical disturbances and physical factors
> ➤ F60–F69 Disorders of adult personality and behavior
> ➤ F70–F79 Intellectual disabilities
> ➤ F80–F89 Pervasive and specific developmental disorders
> ➤ F90–F98 Behavioral and emotional disorders with onset usually occurring in childhood and adolescence
> ➤ F99 Unspecified mental disorder

By looking at these 10 categories of diagnoses (plus the ever-present "unspecified" category, now coded as F99), one can read-ily see where to search for such diagnoses as major depression (Mood [affective] disorders, F30–F39), phobia (Anxiety, dissocia-tive, stress-related, somatoform and other nonpsychotic mental disorders, F40–F48), borderline personality disorder (Disorders of adult personality and behavior, F60–F69), and attention-deficit/hyperactivity disorder (Behavioral and emotional disorders with onset usually occurring in childhood and adolescence, F90–F98).

Two Examples of the Basic Coding Structure of ICD–10–CM

The coding structure is logical. The codes for mental, behavioral, and neurodevelopmental disorders begin with the letter *F,* and numbers are added in an orderly sequence to arrive at a specific diagnosis.

In the first example to follow, the exact diagnostic name or descriptor differs slightly from ICD–9–CM, DSM–IV–TR, and

DSM–5 (American Psychiatric Association, 2013a). F33.2 is the selected diagnostic code. The letter *F* and each number are chosen as follows:

F = Mental, Behavioral, and Neurodevelopmental Disorders
F30–F39 = Mood [affective] disorders
F33 = Major depressive disorder, recurrent
F33.2 = Major depressive disorder, recurrent severe without psychotic features

For comparison purposes, note that 296.33 is the ICD–9–CM code in use until October 2014 for Major depressive disorder, recurrent, without psychotic features. Also for comparison purposes, DSM–5 still codes major depressive disorder, recurrent, severe, according to ICD–9–CM as 296.33; it then gives the ICD–10–CM diagnosis (F33.2) in parenthesis after the ICD–9–CM code. The harmonization of the DSM to fit the ICD coding system works well in this instance. In other words, the old code was 296.33 for ICD–9–CM and DSM–IV–TR; the new code is F33.2 for ICD–10–CM, and DSM–5 offers 296.33 while ICD–9–CM is still in effect and F33.2 for when ICD–10–CM is implemented.

In the next example, the name or descriptor of the diagnosis in ICD–10–CM is exactly the same as in ICD–9–CM, but it is not identical to DSM–IV–TR or DSM–5, in either the name or the coding. F40.01 is the selected diagnostic code.

F = Mental, Behavioral, and Neurodevelopmental Disorders
F40 = Phobic anxiety disorders
F40.0 = Agoraphobia
F40.01 = Agoraphobia with panic disorder

For comparison purposes, note that 300.21 is the ICD–9–CM code in use until October 2014 for this diagnosis. However, there is a disjuncture between the DSM and ICD for this diagnosis. In DSM–IV–TR, 300.21 is the code for panic disorder with agoraphobia—a simple reversal of terms, but both agoraphobia and panic are joined, as they are in ICD–9–CM. However, in DSM–5, they are not. The DSM–5 code for agoraphobia is 300.22 (duplicating the first four digits, but not the fifth, of ICD–9–CM) until next year, and it will be F40.00 (again similar to ICD–10–CM but also with a different fifth digit) when ICD–10–CM is implemented. There is no category that combines agoraphobia with panic disorder in DSM–5. The DSM–5 code for panic disorder to coordinate with ICD–10–CM is F41.0, which corresponds to the ICD–10–CM descriptor for F41.0, Panic disorder without agoraphobia. In this instance, one can see that DSM–5 is not reliably consistent with ICD–10–CM. This is the reason that professionals must understand and use the ICD codes and should not assume the DSM provides a match for ICD codes. One would have to use (and may use) two DSM–5 diagnoses, agoraphobia and panic disorder, which are considered frequently comorbid disorders, to capture the information given in the ICD–10–CM diagnosis of Agoraphobia with panic disorder.

As an alternative to looking up a new code, clinicians who know and understand well the descriptions accompanying the old diagnostic code they are planning to use may turn to conversion tools. One such resource is ICD10Data.com (http://www. icd10data.com/Convert), a free medical coding site where one may enter either an ICD–9–CM or an ICD–10–CM code and locate the conversion from one version to the other.

New Instructional Notes and Conventions

Because ICD–10–CM coding is unlike ICD–9–CM and DSM–IV–TR coding, those readers who have not done so already may wish to look at the Appendix to more readily see how the examples given here are integrated into the new code set.

The *Includes* notes further define or give examples for a category. For instance, F06, the code for Other mental disorders due to known physiological condition, includes mental disorders due to the following: endocrine disorder, exogenous hormone, exogenous toxic substance, primary cerebral disease, somatic illness, and systemic disease affecting the brain. To use an example with fewer inclusions, F18, Inhalant related disorders, includes volatile solvents.

There are two types of *Excludes* notes. One excludes note lists all conditions that cannot be coded at the same time as the primary code because those conditions cannot occur together. The other type of excludes note indicates conditions that are distinct from and not part of the primary code under consideration, but these codes could also be assigned at the same time as the primary code.

Excludes1 means "not coded here." Any conditions listed as Excludes1 codes may not be used with the primary code being considered, because they cannot occur together. For example, F80.1, Expressive language disorder (Developmental dysphasia or aphasia, expressive type), is accompanied by an Excludes1 note. Mixed receptive-expressive language disorder, which would be coded F80.2, may not be used if F80.1 is the primary code. In other words, as common sense would dictate, one may not choose both expressive and mixed receptive-expressive types, and the exclusion note helpfully informs the reader that the code for the mixed receptive-expressive type is F80.2.

Excludes2 means "not included here," because any conditions listed as Excludes2 codes are not part of the condition represented by the code selected. However, these Excludes2 codes may be used in conjunction with the code under consideration. For example, the same code for expressive language disorder just given, F80.1, carries an Excludes2 list of conditions: acquired aphasia with epilepsy (G40.80–), selective mutism (F94.0), intellectual disabilities (F70–F79), and pervasive developmental disorders (F84.–). It is permissible to assign F80.1 and one or more of Excludes2 conditions because the codes listed under Excludes2 are distinct from and not part of the first code. They may occur together (unlike Excludes1 conditions), but they are treated as two separate co-occurring diagnoses. The use of two codes in this instance provides an accurate and specific additive description of the clinical picture.

Code first and *use additional code* notes require that an underlying condition be sequenced first, followed by the manifestation of that condition. For example, the F07 code, Personality and behavioral disorders due to known physiological condition, is accompanied by the instruction to code first "the underlying physiological condition." In another example, F10, Alcohol related disorders, calls for the use of an additional code for "blood alcohol level, if applicable (Y90.–)." In a third example, F70–F79, Intellectual Disabilities, the user is instructed to code first "any associated physical or developmental disorders."

Code also notes are provided where two codes may be required to fully capture a condition. However, the sequencing of the codes depends on severity and the primary reason for the clinical encounter. For example, Speech and language development delay due to hearing loss, F80.4, requires that the type of hearing loss be coded also (H90.–, H91.–), but the order of assigned codes is not specified.

Coding and Reporting Guidelines

The *Official Guidelines for Coding and Reporting* (CDC, 2013b) are intended to complement the instructional notes and conventions described previously. These coding guidelines contain three sections: Section I, "Conventions for the ICD–10–CM" (summarized in the previous section), "General Coding Guidelines" (e.g., locating a code, level of detail, and acute versus chronic conditions), and "Chapter Specific Guidelines" (Chapter 5 is for mental, behavioral, and neurodevelopmental disorders); Section II gives information on the selection of a principal diagnosis; and Section III focuses on reporting additional diagnoses. The guidelines may be found on the CDC website (http://www.cdc.gov/nchs/data/icd9/icd10cm_guidelines_2014.pdf). Most clinicians will have no need to master the details of coding guidelines because knowledge about the proper diagnostic code to select and the conventions to use will be sufficient in most instances. It is helpful, however, to be aware of the guidelines as an additional resource to access as necessary.

Diagnostic Nuances in Coding

Apart from the instructional notes, there are some clinically important nuances used in ICD–10–CM that may not be readily apparent at first glance to those accustomed to the DSM. Such a disjuncture was described in the preceding section on the basic coding structure of ICD–10–CM.

The following example involving persistent anxiety depression is another instance of a mental health symptom picture, which may throw into bolder relief the issue of what may or may not be clinically useful to practitioners. In ICD–10–CM, the diagnosis of Dysthymic disorder, F34.1, encompasses the terms *Depressive neurosis, Depressive personality disorder, Dysthymia, Neurotic depression,* and *Persistent anxiety depression.* When used to code persistent anxiety depression, ICD–10–CM has an Excludes2 note. The diagnosis of anxiety depression ("mild or not persistent") may not be coded with persistent anxiety depression because, obviously, "persistent" and "not persistent" cannot be part of the same condition. It also offers the information that F41.8, Other specified anxiety disorders, is the code to select for anxiety depression that is not persistent. By contrast, the DSM–IV–TR code for dysthymic disorder, 300.4, does not include any associated anxiety in the description of dysthymic symptoms or criteria. In DSM–5, the diagnosis of persistent depressive disorder (dysthymia) is coded the same as it is in ICD–9–CM, 300.4, and in ICD–10–CM, F34.1. The revised DSM–5 diagnosis combines dysthymia and major depressive disorder (chronic). It is not considered a milder form of depression, but rather the chronic form of depression. Also in the reconceptualization, DSM–5 now allows clinicians to specify whether persistent depressive disorder is accompanied by "anxious distress."

These differences may seem small, but they occur for a reason and are not necessarily minor. In DSM–5 trials in the United States, the interrater reliability for the diagnosis of mixed anxiety depression was so low, 0.06, that it is not included as a diagnosis in DSM–5 at all (American Psychological Association, 2013), although the importance of accounting for this mixed clinical picture is addressed to some extent by adding the specifier "with anxious distress" to persistent depressive disorder (dysthymia).

Interestingly, there is a distinct code for Mixed anxiety and depressive disorder, F41.2, in ICD–10, which is intended for use when neither anxiety nor depression predominates but symptoms of both are present (WHO, 2010). This code, F41.2, was removed entirely from the adapted ICD–10–CM version for the U.S. Instead, the diagnostic code for "other specified anxiety disorders," F41.8, encompasses anxiety depression (mild or not persistent), anxiety hysteria, and mixed anxiety and depressive disorder. Although this differs from ICD–10, in which F41.8 includes only anxiety hysteria, it may still be useful that mixed anxiety and depressive disorder is embedded within another code. In contrast, DSM–5 places persistent anxiety depression in the mood disorders category, but places "other specified anxiety disorder" (F41.8), in the anxiety disorders category, and does not contain anxiety depression (mild or not persistent) at all, although it is in ICD–10–CM. Of course, clinicians such as primary care physicians and advanced nurse practitioners, as well as psychologists and other specialist mental health professionals, routinely see people with a mixed clinical picture of both anxiety and depression. WHO intended the inclusion of this category in ICD–10 to aid and promote the diagnostic description of commonly seen distress states that are severe and that interfere with functioning, especially in instances where a traditional psychiatric diagnostic label may not be applicable (WHO, 1992b). WHO recognized that these symptom mixtures often trigger visits for primary care and specialty mental health care services and thus must be accounted for in a clinically useful classification system.

A major ICD revision-related study for the development of ICD–11 examined the ways that clinicians view persistent anxiety depression. This study on the natural ordering of categories by mental health professionals in eight countries (including the United States) found that 95.8% of the clinicians thought mixed anxiety and depressive disorder should be included in a mental disorder classification system (Reed et al., 2013). More of them grouped it with anxiety disorders, although a subset grouped it with mood disorders at levels consistent with the proposals for ICD–11, revealing variability in how clinicians conceptualize this diagnosis. Perhaps some of the variation is influenced by whether patients present more strongly with anxiety or with depression at the outset. Despite the attempts to categorize mixed anxiety and depression, this is one of the diagnoses that remain problematic to classify more precisely, at least for the time being.

Yet, clinicians throughout the world still find the descriptor useful. When psychologists in 23 countries were surveyed, 44% of these experienced clinicians reported using the diagnosis at least once a week in their practices (Evans et al., 2013). Strikingly, there are still unresolved issues surrounding this common mixed condition, which is just one example of the difficulties inherent in any classification system that is used by clinicians who vary widely, with patients who vary widely. We see mixed anxiety depression regularly, we know it, we select it often as a diagnosis, but we cannot quite classify it reliably in the current systems.

Practitioners must use their clinical judgment in selecting the ICD–10–CM diagnosis, or coexisting diagnoses, that represent the best clinical fit among the available choices to describe the patient. The world is not perfect but a classification system is an important tool for communication and treatment planning. However, communication at the clinical level among professionals delivering care is not limited to diagnostic codes. Health care professionals routinely communicate additional clinical information that is needed to modify or enhance an understanding of the clinical condition and the person who has the clinical condition.

Clinical Descriptions and Diagnostic Guidelines

WHO (1992b) published *The ICD–10 Classification of Mental and Behavioural Disorders: Clinical Descriptions and Diagnostic Guidelines*[1] (CDDG), which is known as the *Blue Book,* for use by mental and behavioral health professionals and educators. However, it has been explicitly removed from use in the United States (ADMINDXRW, 2013; and personal communication, March 2013). There are no clinical descriptions accompanying the U.S. modified versions of ICD–9–CM or ICD–10–CM. The U.S. government allows health professionals to use updated diagnostic guidelines and relies on clinicians to use those that are current in their particular area of health practice.

Nevertheless, because the CDDG offers important background information on how classification is approached in the ICD system, and especially because it is being updated for ICD–11, it is important for practitioners to understand the CDDG as a resource to aid in making accurate diagnoses. No doubt when regulatory hearings and comment periods are held on ICD–11 in the United States, there will be strong advocates for the recognition of the new CDDG revision. In the meantime, this section addresses the CDDG and other diagnostic guidelines as well, because clinicians need guidance for making diagnoses beyond just having a code set. A copy of the CDDG may be downloaded from http://www.who.int/classifications/icd/en/bluebook.pdf. It is of interest despite its omission in the United States. There is a different version for researchers, *The ICD–10 Classification of Mental and Behavioural Disorders: Diagnostic Criteria for Research* (the Green Book; WHO, 1993) and yet another shorter version for primary health care workers, *Diagnostic and Management Guidelines for Mental Disorders in Primary Care: ICD–10 Chapter V Primary Care Version* (WHO, 1996).

The CDDG provides explanations for how classification has been approached, especially in what are described as "notoriously difficult" problem areas to describe and classify, such as F23 (Acute and transient psychotic disorders) and F30–F39 (Mood [affective] disorders).

---

[1]WHO uses the spelling *behavioural* in its English language publications; however, in the United States the word is spelled *behavioral,* though the meaning is the same. Throughout this primer, both spellings are used according to their appropriate context.

For each disorder, a description is provided of the main clinical features, and also of any important but less specific associated features. "Diagnostic guidelines" are then provided in most cases, indicating the number and balance of symptoms usually required before a confident diagnosis can be made. The guidelines are worded so that a degree of flexibility is retained for diagnostic decisions in clinical work, particularly in the situation where provisional diagnosis may have to be made before the clinical picture is entirely clear or information is complete. To avoid repetition, clinical descriptions and some general diagnostic guidelines are provided for certain groups of disorders, in addition to those that relate only to individual disorders. (p. 8)

The guidelines are general and flexible, which means that clinical judgment may be brought to bear if the duration of symptoms is longer or shorter than specified or if a "provisional" or "tentative" diagnosis is needed under circumstances of insufficient information for a "confident" diagnosis. This is in contrast to the diagnostic criteria in the DSM system, which requires in many instances a minimum number of symptoms and specified duration. For some disorders, the number of symptoms required is fewer or the duration is shorter in DSM–5 than in DSM–IV–TR. For example, there are relaxed criteria in DSM–5 for attention-deficit/hyperactivity disorder and posttraumatic stress disorder (PTSD).

Criteria and descriptions for diagnoses evolve over time as research and clinical evidence evolve. For some medical conditions, consensus decisions are made periodically to update descriptions as needed. In mental and behavioral health, clinicians may refer to the clinical practice guidelines produced by a number of professional organizations. There are far too many guidelines to discuss in this primer, but it may be helpful to provide a few resources related to reactions to severe stress, as an example. The International Society for Traumatic Stress Studies provides information on trauma assessment for children and adults, as well as clinical practice guidelines from the United States, England, and Australia, on its website (http://www.istss.org/ InternationalPracticeGuidelines.htm). Forbes et al. (2010) evaluated and compared the guidelines for PTSD and related conditions to facilitate practitioner choices about their use and best practices for this diagnosis. In addition, the American Psychological Association is in the process of developing clinical guidelines for PTSD, in addition to guidelines for depression, obesity, and other conditions.

The DSM system has been the predominant resource for mental health diagnostic descriptions in the United States, and research done by many of psychology's clinical scientists contributed to the improvements in DSM–5. Psychologists participated in work groups for some of the diagnostic categories. However, the American Psychiatric Association board of trustees had the authority to reject the recommendations of its work groups, and did so in some instances. For example, the criteria and categories for the ten personality disorders were retained from DSM–IV–TR (American Psychiatric Association, 2013c), although the work group recommendations for dimensional-categorical revisions that were not accepted by the board of trustees are included as an alternative research model for personality disorders in Section III, Emerging Measures and Models. Few of the new disorders in DSM–5, regardless of category, appeared in previous DSM appendices as conditions that required further study. However, other disorders that did appear in such appendices, such as passive–aggressive personality, are not in DSM–5.

For the time being, clinicians may turn to either DSM–IV–TR or DSM–5 for descriptive guidance on ICD diagnostic categories. The American Psychiatric Association (2013b) determines when DSM–IV–TR is obsolete; they expect those who use the DSM for guidance to complete the transition to DSM–5 by January 1, 2014. Yet, the CMS (2013) has ruled that both DSM–IV–TR and DSM–5 are "compatible" with the HIPAA adopted code set, ICD–9–CM, in use until October 2014. After ICD–10–CM is implemented as the official code set on October 1, 2014, DSM–IV–TR will no longer be considered relevant, although it should remain a reasonable resource for clinical descriptors until then. The American Psychiatric Association is promoting their newer product, DSM–5, and they have established the January 1, 2014, date for ending the use of DSM–IV–TR (American Psychiatric Association, 2013b).

In some settings, clinicians have long been required to follow DSM criteria for diagnoses, and administrators in these settings may mandate the use of DSM–5 too. The use of a diagnostic system parallel to the ICD for a subset of diseases and disorders in the United States is only possible due to the harmonization efforts at the government level. In the past, the DSM has been synchronized reasonably well with the ICD; there are few (albeit significant) differences between the codes of ICD–9–CM and DSM–IV–TR, due to the efforts of NCHS in working with the American Psychiatric Association to make the ICD clinical modification version for the United States and the DSM consistent (Reed, 2010). The new DSM–5 attempts to both closely parallel the disorder codes in ICD–10–CM and also align in some respects with the forthcoming significantly revised ICD–11 structure for disorders (Kupfer, Kuhl, & Regier, 2013). Thus, the American Psychiatric Association has tried to bridge ICD–9–CM, ICD–10–CM, and ICD–11 in its 947-page DSM–5.

WHO has expressed concern about the proliferation of mental and behavioral diagnoses and the questionable diagnostic categories that exist today (Reed, Dua, & Saxena, 2011). Citing Moynihan (2011), Reed, Dua, et al. (2011) supported the proposition that the definition of disease "cannot be legitimately managed by a single professional organization representing a single health discipline in a single country with a substantial commercial investment in its products." They recognized the important contributions that government organizations (e.g., National Institutes of Health in the United States and National Institute for Health and Care Excellence in the United Kingdom) and professional, disease, and consumer organizations make to disease definition. But they also reminded us that WHO, in its constitutionally mandated role, sets the disease definition standards and coordinates multilateral global action.

The ICD system has historically provided guidance to clinicians though the CDDG (described at the beginning of this section), which is designed to fit the ICD system. It is a loss not to have this guidance in an updated form released simultaneously with the adoption of ICD–10–CM in the United States. But it will likely be available again to clinicians for ICD–11; the revised and updated CDDG will accompany the release of ICD–11 in 2014. It should provide valuable clinical descriptions for making diagnoses within the ICD system, and we expect there will be no grounds for its exclusion in the United States. For further explanation, see the preview of ICD–11 in Chapter 5.

Diagnostic Code Changes and Incompatibilities

Attempts have been made to harmonize DSM with ICD in creating ICD–10–CM, generally in the direction of trying to keep DSM–IV–TR diagnoses for mental health categories. As a result, there are coding incompatibilities between ICD–10 and its clinical modification version for the United States, especially in the area of substance-related diagnoses. For example, ICD–10–CM uses a complex system that combines substance use disorders (e.g., dependence and abuse) with the consequences of those disorders (e.g., withdrawal and substance-induced psychosis); this has been done to preserve the conventions used in ICD–9–CM and DSM–IV–TR terminology (First & Reed, 2013).

Also, most disorders included in ICD–10, but not the DSM, have been omitted in ICD–10–CM at the recommendation, for the most part, of the American Psychiatric Association (First & Reed, 2013). For example, the ICD–10 code for mixed anxiety and depression disorder, F41.2, discussed at some length in a previous section, is not in ICD–10–CM. The code set skips from F41.1 to F41.3. Mixed anxiety and depression is subsumed under "other specified anxiety disorders." Conversely, some diagnoses included in DSM–5, such as disruptive mood dysregulation disorder, are not included in ICD–10–CM. This had been named "temper dysregulation disorder with dysphoria" earlier in the DSM–5 development process and met with widespread complaints that spilled over into the general media (e.g., Dobbs, 2012). Concerns about normal children with temper tantrums being diagnosed with a mental health condition were expressed. Despite the brouhaha in the media, the reasoning behind this new diagnosis of disruptive mood dysregulation disorder is worth consideration.

The goal of the DSM–5 work groups and task force was to lessen the likelihood of overdiagnosing and overtreating children under the age of 18 for bipolar disorder (American Psychiatric Association, 2013a). However, it would be unprecedented to add a new diagnosis to the HIPAA-approved code set (ICD–10–CM) on the basis of the need to reduce the incidence of overprescribing medications for children. There may be other ways to achieve this valuable goal than through a diagnostic taxonomy system. Nevertheless, when the freeze on any changes to ICD–10–CM expires, the American Psychiatric Association may ask for the inclusion of disruptive mood dysregulation disorder, along with other modifications based on new DSM–5 diagnoses not included in ICD–10–CM.

For busy clinicians who do not want to memorize the differences between the ICD and DSM and who may not track the modifications process closely, it is sufficient to remember the basic rule: Use an ICD–10–CM code if you are billing a third-party payer. If it is not in ICD–10–CM, the claim will be rejected.

General Equivalence Mappings

General Equivalence Mappings (GEMs) are translation reference maps published by NCHS to compare code classifications between ICD–9–CM and ICD–10–CM. These GEMs are intended for large data repositories, not for general clinical use. But, because clinicians may hear about them in many venues where the ICD is discussed, a brief sketch may provide a useful summary.

Because of the major changes between the two versions of ICD–CM, an ordinary crosswalk between ICD–9–CM and ICD–10–CM would be viewed as inaccurate for major institutional, state, and national data-gathering purposes. It is not feasible to say that a specific code in ICD–9–CM is always equivalent to one particular code in ICD–10–CM, because there are only about 14,000 codes in Version 9, and there are approximately 68,000 codes in Version 10. This translates into 54,000 more coding options available in the newer version. Therefore, GEMs have been created to provide suggestions, not answers that could be considered a one-to-one equivalence—in other words, they provide the "raw material" for users to derive results specific to their needs (Giannangelo, 2011).

A particular diagnostic code that appears in one version of the ICD may be only an approximation, rather than an equivalent match, in the other version. For those working with large data sets, such as researchers and epidemiologists, GEMs are useful because they are bidirectional. A *source system* is the original code set that is being mapped from; a *target system* is the destination code set being mapped to (Giannangelo, 2011). The purpose of GEMs is to preserve the continuity of health information over the years so that it is not disrupted by the transition from ICD–9–CM to ICD–10–CM. Information can be mapped forward from ICD–9–CM to ICD–10–CM or backward from ICD–10–CM to ICD–9–CM.

Practitioners have no need to use GEMs. It is easier to just look up a needed diagnostic code in Chapter 5 ("Mental, Behavioral, and Neurodevelopmental Disorders") of ICD–10–CM or use an approximated crosswalk or conversion application that suits the purpose.

Electronic Billing

In anticipation of the change to ICD–10–CM, all electronic billing systems have to be updated to comply with HIPAA regulations. The newer Version 5010 for electronic administrative transactions, which went into effect in 2012, supports both the ICD–9 and ICD–10 code structures (CMS, 2012a). The HIPAA standards have been updated, and they include claims, eligibility, and authorizations for referral. Practitioners in most settings will be current already, but for anyone who is making the transition to a new electronic billing service, it is best to inquire about the vendor's Version 5010 compliance status. If a given system does not support the latest version, claims will be rejected. It is important to note that the clearinghouses that handle billing transactions will not convert ICD–9–CM to ICD–10–CM for providers. The computer software used for creating the transaction bills has to be compliant before the bills for treatment are transmitted to a clearinghouse.

Electronic health record templates may also need changes to be consistent with ICD–10–CM requirements. Professionals who use practice management software for billing and clinical records will need to consult with the software developers about their timetables and readiness to make the necessary transition. There will be costs involved with updating the software as well, and these are likely to be passed along to the users of the systems.

Relationship Between the ICD and the ICF

The *International Classification of Functioning, Disability, and Health* (ICF; WHO, 2001) remains unfamiliar to many psychologists. It is a companion classification for ICD–10 that is related to health and mental health and designed to assess and categorize function. From a biopsychosocial perspective, the ICF classifies function, not disease. Its value lies in helping practitioners to gain a more complete clinical picture of a patient to better plan individually tailored treatment.

The ICF describes how people live with a health condition, including mental health, and it classifies health-related domains and some health-related components of well-being. The system encompasses personal, social, and environmental factors that affect function. It also provides a framework on which assessment tools may be based, although it is important to remember the ICF is a classification system and not a measurement instrument. For measurement, WHO produces the *WHO Disability Assessment Schedule 2.0* (WHODAS; 2013c). It is available in five languages, and there are many more translations underway. WHODAS is a generic measure that can be used across all diseases (including mental, neurological, and substance abuse disorders) and in adults across all cultures. It is directly linked, conceptually, to the ICF. The six domains assessed are (a) cognition, (b) mobility, (c) self-care, (d) getting along (interacting with other people), (e) life activities (including work, home, and school responsibilities, as well as leisure pursuits), and (f) participation (e.g., community involvement). Different versions of the WHODAS questionnaires may be downloaded (see http://www.who.int/classifications/icf/whodasii/en/). Of course, one may use other measures of function too.

Psychologists should be interested in the ICF because it addresses how patients truly function in the world. In the past, I have discussed the importance and the potential of the ICF for U.S. practitioners (Goodheart, 2011) because function is an ever-present focus in clinicians' daily work. The ICF is meant to be used in varying clinical settings with varying assessment procedures. It orients services and outcomes toward function instead of simply toward symptom reduction. It can help clinicians begin to understand differences in functional status and targets for intervention from the outset (Lynn Bufka, personal communication, 2010). This is relevant to psychologists who are focusing increasingly on areas such as patients' productivity, recovery, resilience, well-being, and thriving. Practitioners are required to be increasingly accountable and to obtain consistently good outcomes, while delivering services "efficiently" under the watchful eye of the developing accountable care organizations. To meet these goals, practitioners will need greater latitude to target both function and disorder, and they will need readily accessible and inexpensive clinical tools to do so. The ICD and ICF and WHODAS are all WHO resources that are freely available and designed to work together.

Process for Changes to ICD–10–CM

During the freeze period until October 1, 2015, and afterward, changes to ICD–10–CM are likely to be recommended by the creator of DSM–5, the American Psychiatric Association, to maintain consistency between the two diagnostic systems. It is not certain whether all suggestions will actually be adopted. To make changes, there is a lengthy public process that includes government agency posting of suggested changes, professional reviews and public feedback, hearings, and rulemaking. The American Psychological Association and the American Psychological Association Practice Organization will monitor the process. They will offer suggestions and commentary, as they do in all matters of importance to the profession of psychology, to mental and behavioral health services, and to public welfare. Psychologists have an essential stake in how ICD–10–CM is changed, as well as how soon the United States adopts ICD–11 and its updated CDDG. In the end, despite not knowing in advance all the details of how ICD–10–CM will evolve, it is unlikely that clinicians will have difficulty in locating the most frequently used diagnostic codes that are applicable to the patients they treat.

Chapter 4

Strengths and Limitations of Diagnostic Classification

There are many ways to organize a diagnostic classification system. No one has yet found the ideal solution, if such a thing exists, although much thought and conscientious work have gone into improving the mechanisms available to clinicians and researchers. To establish systems that are reliable, valid, and feasible for use in ordinary clinical settings, developers have considered many approaches, including descriptive, criteria-based, dimensional rating, and prototype matching models.

The *International Classification of Diseases* (ICD; World Health Organization [WHO], 1992a) and *Diagnostic and Statistical Manual of Mental Disorders* (DSM) systems, which have shown improved reliability in research settings over time, both use a descriptive, criteria-based approach to diagnosis. The ICD uses more general descriptive diagnostic guidelines with some flexibility for fluid clinical situations, whereas the DSM uses more categorically defined criteria that are stricter and establish a minimum number of symptoms and duration of symptoms.

Improvements

Despite the lack of major breakthroughs, incremental improvements are seen in ICD–10–CM (Centers for Disease Control and Prevention [CDC], 2013). It is an upgrade from the obsolete ICD–9–CM (CDC, 2011), although it must be emphasized that the forthcoming restructured ICD–11, in comparison with

ICD–10–CM or DSM–5 (American Psychiatric Association, 2013a), will better represent the ways in which clinicians conceptualize and organize diagnoses (Roberts et al., 2012). Nevertheless, ICD–10–CM, with its large increase in the number of codes available and room to add more as needed, offers a broader range of content, updated descriptors, and greater clinical detail than is available in ICD–9–CM.

The greatest benefits of ICD–10–CM accrue mainly to those who aggregate and analyze large amounts of health data; it is less beneficial to mental and behavioral health professionals who treat patients. For example, as discussed in Chapter 3 of this primer, the National Center for Health Statistics predicted the improved data will permit better measurement of care, payment system design, claim processing, public health tracking, fraud detection, and the conduct of research (Pickett, 2012). Adoption of ICD–10–CM will be beneficial to the United States for reporting and comparing international morbidity and mortality data. Therefore, a public health benefit is expected. This is a meaningful improvement.

The reason for less expected gain at the clinical level is that ICD–10 (WHO, 1992a), on which ICD–10–CM is based, is now more than 20 years old. WHO is undertaking its revision to create ICD–11 because the World Health Assembly considers ICD–10 outdated. For those medical specialties without sufficient codes to stay current with changes in medical diagnosis and practice, ICD–10–CM, with its greatly increased number of codes, may be a boon. Mental health professionals have struggled more with issues of accuracy and the clinical usefulness of its codes rather than a need for more codes. Yet all clinicians will benefit over time from the improved fit with computerized coding technology.

Clinical Utility Issues

The clinical utility of mental disorders classification in ICD–10, DSM–IV–TR (American Psychiatric Association, 2000), and DSM–5 has been criticized rather extensively (Andrews et al., 2009; First, 2010; Hansen et al., 2013; Kendell & Jablensky, 2003; Reed, 2010). Michael First (2010) described clinical utility as enhanced when four goals for a classification system are met, helping clinicians to

> **(1)** *communicate* **clinical information to other practitio-
> ners, to patients and their families, and to health care**

systems administrators; (2) *implement effective interventions* **in order to improve clinical outcomes; (3)** *predict the future* **in terms of clinical management needs and likely outcomes, and (4)** *differentiate disorder from non-disorder* **for the purpose of determining who might benefit from disorder-based treatments. (p. 466)**

This is an excellent description of a practice-friendly classification system.

Examining classification systems that are not practice-friendly, Geoffrey Reed (2010), WHO's senior project officer for the development of the new "Mental, Behavioural and Neurodevelopmental Disorders" chapter in ICD–11, addressed the problem of clinical utility directly. In particular, he singled out four indicators of the weaknesses in the current diagnostic systems (p. 459). First, many mental disorders are coded as "unspecified" (the ICD term) or "not otherwise specified" (the DSM term), which suggests difficulty in use, inaccurate descriptors, or a lack of practicality for fine-grade distinctions. Second, many people meet criteria for two or more disorders, which suggests that the systems do not capture efficiently the nature of clinical presentations of disorders. Third, many treatments (both psychological and pharmacological) are effective across several disorders, which suggests that some diagnostic distinctions may not be clinically relevant. Fourth, many diagnostic categories are not good predictors of treatment, especially for the severely mentally ill, which suggests that the current systems are not supporting the wise use of the limited available treatment resources in many settings.

Furthermore, although the hierarchical decimal coding format of ICD–10–CM is easy to understand and the conversion charts and applications will make it easy to find the diagnosis one seeks, psychopathology does not naturally present and arrange itself within hierarchical groups of 10. The structure has artificial or forced hierarchies containing diagnostic categories that do not naturally fit together (Reed, 2012, Slide 10). For example,

> ➢ F40–F48, Anxiety, dissociative, stress-related, somatoform, and other nonpsychotic mental disorders. This category combines differing clinical phenomena such as phobias, adjustment disorders, and body dysmorphic disorder.

> F50–F59, Behavioral syndromes associated with physiological disturbances and physical factors. This category encompasses disparate diagnoses such as eating disorders, insomnia, sexual dysfunction, and postpartum depression. Although all have physical manifestations, it seems highly unlikely these disorders are etiologically related.
> F60–F69, Disorders of adult personality and behavior. This category contains all the personality disorders, together with pathological gambling and trichotillomania, gender identity disorders, and factitious disorder. It is difficult to see this grouping as cohesive.

In discussing the clinical utility that is associated with diagnosing problems in different populations, Helena Hansen et al. (2013) criticized DSM–5 for omitting the social determinants of disorders and diagnoses, pointing out that it lacks a systematic method for consideration of population level variations in diagnoses. On the basis of their assessment, they proposed the creation of an independent diagnosis review body to apply appropriate population health and social science research lessons to improve the DSM. Although recognizing the need for and the merit of improving clinical utility, we know the task is not an easy one. The developers of ICD–11 are working toward it assiduously in promising steps and field studies that are presented in the next chapter.

Reliability and Validity Problems

In the search for greater accuracy, those who develop diagnostic classification systems such as ICD–10, ICD–10–CM, DSM–IV–TR, and DSM–5 may have gone too far in terms of specificity, often leaving practitioners to grapple with a poor fit between the clinical presentations of their patients and the codes by which they must describe them. The systems may have achieved reasonable reliability in research settings—although reliability has been poorer in practice settings—but validity has proved to be more elusive and remains a problem (Garb, 2005; Hyman, 2010; Insel, 2013). Developers hoped that increasingly reliable descriptive symptom-based classification would lead to gains in validity, but those gains have not materialized. WHO is well aware of the absence of compelling validity data for classification systems, which is the reason the ICD–10 revision process leading to ICD–11 is focused principally on improving clinical utility.

The reliability of DSM–5 has been called into question primarily because the interrater reliability standards for diagnoses have been lowered based on field trial results in clinical settings. Before discussing the disappointing kappa coefficients for commonly occurring diagnoses, a refresher on the meaning of this statistic may be useful for some readers. A kappa coefficient of 1 means perfect agreement among two or more raters, and a kappa coefficient of 0 means the agreement is equivalent to chance (Viera & Garrett, 2005). It is a conservative statistic, one used to ensure that the agreement is not due merely to chance. DSM–5 lowered its standard from kappa values of 0.6 or above in previous DSMs to ranges of 0.4–0.6 (deemed good for DSM–5) and 0.2–0.4 (deemed acceptable), which was a surprising turn of events (American Psychological Association [APA], 2013). This shows weakness in the field trials, compounded by the fact that not all of the planned trials were completed.

To highlight the drop in interrater reliability over time, consider that for DSM–5, the kappa value for major depressive disorder is 0.32, compared with 0.59 in DSM–IV–TR and 0.80 in DSM–III (American Psychiatric Association, 1980); the value for generalized anxiety disorder is 0.20, compared with 0.65 in DSM–IV–TR and 0.72 in DSM–III (APA, 2013). To be fair, one must also note that the interrater reliability coefficients of many medical conditions in clinical settings are also poor. This is not a problem limited to mental and behavioral conditions; it may be an artifact of the differences between the clinical settings, with all of their variety and comorbidities, and the controlled research conditions in which the diagnoses being tested are limited, the testers are specialists in the particular areas being evaluated, the patients with comorbid conditions are excluded, and other limiting factors are built into the process. In sum, it is easier to obtain reliability under research conditions than it is in the field.

Recognizing the validity and reliability limitations of the DSM diagnostic classification system, the U.S. National Institute of Mental Health (NIMH) announced the establishment of the Research Domain Criteria (RDoC) project (Insel, 2013). It will incorporate genetics, imaging, cognitive science, and other information, to lay the foundation for a new nosology—that is, a new medical classification system. Thomas Insel (2013), the NIMH director, pointed out that although symptom-based diagnosis has been largely replaced in the rest of medicine because "symptoms alone rarely indicate the best choice of treatment," the DSM–5 diagnoses remain based on symptom clusters. Although Insel did not mention the ICD system in the announcement, it is likely his concerns apply to ICD–10–CM as well, given that DSM–5 is harmonized with it.

One of the assumptions underlying the RDoC approach is that a diagnosis should be based on biology as well as symptoms, and the project will not be constrained by the current DSM categories. However, RDoC provides a research framework, not a clinical one. This is expected to be a 10-year effort, which makes any outcomes relevant to patients and practitioners hard to predict. The goal is precision-based mental health diagnosis and treatment that is on par with that of cancer diagnosis and treatment. The goal is laudable, yet it is unclear how a precision medicine approach, which is largely medication based, will be able to address the significant psychosocial, cultural, and environmental issues that are intertwined with brain chemistry issues.

In some ways, the biological approach seems promising, but at the same time, a strictly biological approach seems to favor nature over nurture once again, when the two are inseparable to such a great extent. Social determinants can be pivotal in mental and behavioral disorders. Personal and cultural attitudes toward mental phenomena are influential, whether the phenomena are biologically determined or not. Gene expression may vary considerably from person to person because biological tendencies interact with life experiences and coalesce into individual expressions (e.g., Taylor et al., 2000).

There are no final answers to the big questions surrounding diagnostic classification. We can expect there will be much continuing debate about the best ways to understand and categorize mental and behavioral problems. In the meantime, clinicians must continue to treat patients using the best resources available to them.

Diagnostic Case Formulation—More Than Choosing a Diagnostic Code

Throughout this primer, the discussion has focused primarily on assisting clinicians to understand the changes in the ICD systems. However, the process of arriving at a meaningful diagnosis is a different endeavor than selecting a diagnostic code. A code is merely a tool, although it is obviously an important one. A code provides a mechanism for recording and communicating an understanding of a person's mental and behavioral health condition(s). Making a diagnosis requires clinical acumen and expertise to understand a patient's health status (including mental and behavioral health) within his or her personal context.

Definition

Case formulation may be defined as a conceptualization or a hypothesis that organizes the causes, precipitants, and influences that maintain a person's problems (Eells, 2007). It enables the clinician to better understand a person holistically, by taking into account the complex interactions among internal and environmental forces, as well as the sometimes-contradictory clinical information that informs the overall picture. This definition is atheoretical; in other words, it is not beholden to any particular therapeutic school or orientation. Tracy Eells's (2007) view of case formulation is broad. Within Eells's described blueprint, a clinician may add to and consolidate information about the problem, resolve inconsistencies, and unify historical antecedents and development with current circumstances and function. One uses it to guide treatment and improve the therapeutic alliance as the patient and therapist come to agree on common language for understanding the problem and addressing it.

Case formulation is often influenced by the particular theoretical orientation of the clinician, however. There are several good handbooks and texts on diagnostic case formulation that readers may want to consult; for example, Eells (2007) and Sturmey (2009) presented multiple examples from different orientations, Hersen and Rosqvist (2008) offered a cognitive–behavioral orientation, Sturmey (2008) provided a behavioral orientation, McWilliams (1994) and the *Psychodynamic Diagnostic Manual* (PDM) Task Force (2006) framed a psychodynamic and psychoanalytic orientation, and Ingram (2011) presented an integrative orientation.

In discussing definitions that have been put forward by authors with various theoretical orientations, Sturmey (2009) identified four common features among them: (a) formulations explain essential features of the case and are not merely summaries of details; (b) they integrate case information about problem onset, development, and maintenance into a unified set of ideas that can be linked to treatment; (c) they are provisional in nature and are subject to revision as new information accumulates; and (d) their purpose is to guide treatment that is tailored for the specific patient, to be more effective than a generic treatment would be.

Overall, rigidity seems to be the enemy of good case formulation. Expert clinicians keep an open mind as they "chunk" information and identify patterns. Their case formulations have boundaries, but a formulation is not fixed permanently, and its boundaries may be rearranged in the face of new information. As clinicians, we attempt to hold a sufficiently detailed mental map to offer meaningful treatment without getting lost in excessive detail and losing the essential patient schema. The case formulation fundamentally drives the treatment.

Process

The primary method for beginning to craft a carefully formulated diagnosis is to listen to the patient's narrative closely and synthesize a great deal of clinical information. The process of observing and listening and synthesizing information about a person one has just met takes time and attention to do it well and not foreclose the process prematurely. In addition to a clinical interview, screening tools and psychometric instruments are typically used to assess diverse areas. Depending on the psychologist's patient population and treatment specialty, one chooses different measures to capture clinically relevant information. Some examples of commonly measured domains are symptom distress and comorbidity, social role function and cognitive function, personality and psychopathology, development, acculturation, substance use, suicide risk, readiness to change, physical pain, and quality of life. Some measures capture several domains in one instrument, which is useful for clinicians who are not likely to have more than a limited number of measures on hand. Geropsychologists use different measures than child psychologists, of course. They may be assessing different domains of function, as well as different life stage factors.

It is important to hear the patient's presenting concerns in his or her own words. Embedded in those words are the patient's perceptions and attitudes toward her or his behavior, symptoms, daily function, emotions, thoughts, stressors, relationships, socioeconomic status, and the multiple phenomena occurring within themselves and within their family, social, and school or work networks. Patients also communicate or withhold information (verbally and/or on baseline measures) depending on their perceptions of the clinician. In practice, we learn that our manner, our surroundings, our receptivity and responsiveness to them as unique individuals all have an impact on the potential for a therapeutic alliance that builds trust and facilitates progress. If it takes more than the "initial evaluation" time allotted in a particular setting to develop a formulation, it is reasonable to dedicate further exploration time at the next appointment to fully grasp the complexities and arrive at a diagnostic picture of the priorities to be addressed in treatment. Sometimes the only good choice after the initial meeting is a provisional diagnosis.

A thoughtful diagnostic formulation has major implications for the success of the treatment that follows it. Treatment based on thorough case formulation does not imply the simple selection of a particular set of interventions to use for a particular disorder. Comorbidities are the rule, not the exception to the rule. Clinicians rarely deal with one simple diagnosis in the real world. A patient may fit multiple diagnostic categories, such as major depression, alcohol abuse, and borderline personality disorder. Alternatively, a patient may fit the criteria for one or two diagnoses and also have features of other diagnoses that do not rise to the level of a diagnosable disorder in those categories. Our formulated understanding of a patient will affect the tone we use to introduce interventions, the way we relate to the person, and even the topics we choose to emphasize at the outset (McWilliams, 1994).

Arriving at a diagnosis and tying it to treatment draw on both a practitioner's scientific knowledge base and clinical reality. Clinical realities are more complicated and fluid than the available diagnostic categories, which are hard and fast and often remain so for decades. Over time, practitioners gain a better sense of how symptoms and traits fit into actual lives and how psychological problems affect daily function and relationships at home and at work. As treatment progresses, skilled practitioners revisit the guiding formulation when circumstances such as lack of progress or new clinical information warrant it.

Learning to Make a Diagnosis

Clinicians become good diagnosticians by doing a lot of diagnosis and doing it systematically. Graduate students learn how to formulate diagnoses through many channels in their early phases of training, in addition to assigned readings and exposure to the

ICD and DSM systems. For example, the faculty for the adult psychopathology course at the Rutgers Graduate School of Applied and Professional Psychology (Jamie Walkup, personal communication, July 10, 2013) makes use of vignettes, live interviews, taped interviews, and exercises such as writing up a character in a movie and analyzing a first-person written account of a mental illness by breaking down the clinical information in a structured format. There are many variations in teaching methods, but the great majority of doctoral programs seem to recognize that learning case formulation skills for mental and behavioral disorders is challenging for students.

Barbara Ingram (2003), in a conference poster session on teaching clinical graduate students at the Pepperdine University School of Education and Psychology, presented two educational objectives: the acquisition of 33 case formulation skills and the application of 28 core hypotheses to clinical case information. The task can seem daunting, but Ingram divided it into manageable steps. The formulation skill topic areas include problem identification, outcome goals, database presentation, explanatory discussion, and treatment planning. Clinical hypotheses are organized into seven categories: (a) biological bases; (b) crisis, stressful situations, and transitions; (c) social, cultural, and environmental factors; perspectives based on (d) cognitive, (e) behavior and learning, (f) psychodynamic, and (g) existential and spiritual models. In essence, Ingram described clinical hypotheses as raw ingredients that are used to create a complex recipe, which is called a case formulation.

When speaking to graduate students, I often tell them they are not expected to be experts when they finish graduate school. It takes at least a decade to function at a true expert level, and they should not be discouraged by the mistakes they make (e.g., Goodheart, 2006). However, the accumulation of experience alone does not necessarily produce expertise; something else is needed. Eells, Lombart, Kendjelic, Turner, and Lucas (2005) compared expert, experienced, and novice therapists on the quality of their case formulations. The experts' formulations were more comprehensive, elaborated, and complex than the other groups; their treatment plans were more developed and a better fit for the formulations; they made more use of systematic reasoning; they elaborated more on possible diagnoses, global functioning problems, inferred problems, and psychological mechanisms. Their total quality ratings were superior. In a finding that might seem surprising to some people, the novices were more highly rated on total formulation quality than the experienced group (but not the expert group). The study authors reasoned that the experts keep themselves highly calibrated to a standard, and the novices are newly calibrated by the recency of their training; however, the experienced therapists are more distant from both training and case formulation experiences and may not be aware of the need to recalibrate and resharpen this skill set. There were few differences between therapists of varied theoretical orientations. This finding is in line with the conclusions of Wiser and Goldfried (1998), who found expert therapists with different orientations were similar in their explorations of patients' emotionally significant events.

Conceptualization in Evidence-Based Practice

In the report of the APA Presidential Task Force on Evidence-Based Practice (2006), the section on clinical expertise describes the clinical skills needed to make a diagnosis and develop an appropriate treatment plan in order to be of significant benefit to the person seeking help:

> The clinically expert psychologist is able to formulate clear and theoretically coherent case conceptualizations, assess patient pathology as well as clinically relevant strengths, understand complex patient presentations, and make accurate diagnostic judgments. Expert clinicians revise their case conceptualizations as treatment proceeds and seek both confirming and disconfirming evidence. Clinical expertise also involves identifying and helping patients to acknowledge psychological processes that contribute to distress or dysfunction. Treatment planning involves setting goals and tasks of treatment that take into consideration the unique patient, the nature of the patient's problems and concerns, the likely prognosis and expected benefits of treatment, and available resources. The goals of therapy are developed in collaboration with the patient and consider the patient and his or her family's worldview and sociocultural context. (p. 276)

Summary Thoughts on Making a Diagnosis Versus Choosing a Diagnostic Code

When making a diagnosis, we probably all do well to remind ourselves that the clinical phenomena patients present to us are real. No one wants to be defined as a human being by a reductionist label or category. Our patients want to be understood holistically. Our organization of all the clinical data into a coherent case formulation is the key to matching a treatment plan to the needs and capacities of the patient. The diagnostic codes selected then become a "shorthand" communication tool used to explain the essence of a person's struggles via a set of numbers and letters. To complete the picture, an essential part of the diagnostic process is establishing a therapeutic alliance based on developing shared goals, agreement on the treatment approach and tasks, and a positive emotional bond; all of these elements contribute to positive outcomes of treatment (Horvath & Bedi, 2002; Miller, Duncan, & Hubble, 2005).

Questions for Future Resolution

Any discussion about the strengths and limitations of classification systems would be incomplete without framing important questions that remain open to debate and further research. Michael C. Roberts and Spencer Evans (2013) summarized a number of issues about classification systems that have been raised but are not yet resolved (p. 75): Is there developmental discontinuity between childhood and adult disorders, and how should criteria be tailored for different ages (e.g., child and adult depression or child conduct disorders and adult personality disorders)? Are disorders and criteria sufficiently culturally universal and comprehensive to fit diverse clinical presentations and contexts? Is a categorical or dimensional or combination approach more valid, reliable, and feasible clinically? What is the best way to address the problem of excessive diagnosis of comorbidity? How does one decide to include or exclude diagnoses in a classification system? How can classification systems be improved for greater clinical utility? These are thoughtful questions. The next chapter addresses the final question in the list. It is the question of greatest salience to practicing psychologists.

CHAPTER **5**

Preview of ICD–11

Implementation of the 11th edition of the *International Classification of Diseases* (ICD–11) will be mandatory for the World Health Organization (WHO) member countries after it is adopted by the World Health Assembly (WHA) in 2015. As is customary, it will take some time for country-level modification and implementation, and it is uncertain how long the lag time will be in the United States. It seems improbable that the delays will be as great as they were for the United States' adoption of ICD–10–CM (Centers for Disease Control and Prevention, 2013; remembering that ICD–10 [WHO, 1992] has been used widely throughout the rest of the world for almost 20 years), because there will be pressure to conform more quickly and greater tools to do so. More likely, there will be an incremental process to align ICD–10–CM and ICD–11. Although mental and behavioral health professionals (not to mention the employees of the large government and private insurers and health systems) may dislike the thought of making yet another set of changes to their record keeping, billing, and reporting systems, the changes in ICD–11 should make it well worth the effort.

Once ICD–11 is adopted as the revised world standard, it will benefit the United States to adopt it in a timely way. As a WHO member nation, the United States will be obligated to use ICD–11. Moreover, there are now experts from the U.S. National Committee on Vital Health Statistics participating in the WHO Family of International Classification Network (Reed, 2010), which enhances development and information sharing. Also, WHO expects that updates may be incorporated regularly, perhaps annually through update mechanisms, without the upheaval of a major revision every decade or two (Reed, 2010). Advances in global communication and technology make it possible to incorporate new knowledge at a faster pace. The public health costs, and perhaps financial costs, to the United States for not keeping up with incremental updates to the world standard may have greater consequences than in the past, when the revision process was done on a large scale, decade by decade.

Adoption of ICD–11 will benefit clinicians also, in addition to its enhancement of U.S. health systems. Because frontline practitioners must rely on good diagnostic formulations that are paired with solid clinical descriptions, the diagnostic system chosen as the practitioner's reference point makes a difference. The new architecture of ICD–11 will offer greater clinical accuracy, ease of use, and goodness of fit, all of which should be readily apparent even before the revised system is released.

International Union of Psychological Science and American Psychological Association Involvement

The WHA directed WHO to undertake the revision of ICD–10 after the longest period in ICD history without an update. The multiyear process will result in ICD–11, which as noted previously is planned for adoption by WHA in 2015 after the technical preparation steps are completed in 2014. For the first time, psychologists are involved in an ICD revision, specifically for the content areas related to mental and behavioral disorders. Geoffrey Reed, a psychologist, serves as the senior project officer for the Revision of ICD–10 Mental and Behavioural Disorders, in the Department of Mental Health and Substance Abuse at WHO, Geneva, Switzerland.

As project director, Reed oversees the activities and technical work of the revision. This includes the review of scientific evidence for the revision, the nomination and management of 15 expert working groups and their participation in creating drafts, production of successive drafts, and the design and management of field trials and studies. He is the WHO secretariat member for the International Advisory Group for the Revision of the ICD–10 Mental and Behavioral Disorders and managing editor for the publication of ICD–11 classification of mental and behavioral disorders.

The International Union of Psychological Science (IUPsyS), which is psychology's international organizational representative in relations with WHO, is supporting the revision, with contract funding for the work provided to IUPsyS by the American Psychological Association (APA). Other national psychological associations around the globe have also contributed resources to support and enhance the revision.

Psychologist readers may be curious about why the APA decided to invest in ICD–11.[1] Suzanne Bennett Johnson (APA 2011 President-Elect) summarized the reasons for APA's support in a presentation at the association's annual convention:

> ➢ It is the world's classification system.
> ➢ It is a product of a serious mission on the part of WHO, one that is consistent with APA's mission.
> ➢ Psychologists were invited by WHO to participate.
> ➢ It is free and available worldwide.
> ➢ It is based on multinational data.
> ➢ It is free of commercial influence.
> ➢ It is the official HIPAA approved U.S. system for all third-party billing.
> ➢ It is required by federal regulations for Medicare claims.
> ➢ ICD is created by WHO, whereas the DSM is a product of the American Psychiatric Association, has an Anglophone character, is a proprietary resource of the relatively small organization, and is voted on by their board of trustees.

Psychology, as a discipline, has been more involved in the planning and processes for the ICD–11 chapter on mental and behavioral disorders than for any previous revision. Psychologists have contributed to the research basis for the revision. Psychologists' attitudes toward mental health disorders classification have been surveyed internationally, in multiple languages. Psychologists have also been well represented in the Field Studies Coordinating

---

[1]Author disclosure statement: I was the 2010 APA president and supported the association's involvement in the ICD–11 development throughout my term of office in the presidential cycle (2009–2011) and in the years prior to that as an officer on the board of directors.

Group that guides the development and contributes to testing clinical utility.

Major Aims and Updated Clinical Descriptions and Guidelines

The stated goals of WHO's Department of Mental Health and Substance Abuse for the ICD–11 are to (a) incorporate the advances and changes in scientific knowledge and clinical practice of the last 20 years; (b) improve its effectiveness as a mechanism for reducing disease burden and disability globally; (c) improve the classification system as a diagnostic tool by improving its clinical utility for daily practice, including in primary care, in all countries; and (d) ensure that ICD–11 and health system information technology are compatible (Ritchie, 2013).

Three versions will be derived from the chapter on mental, behavioral, and neurodevelopmental disorders of ICD–11: one for clinical specialty settings (*Clinical Descriptions and Diagnostic Guidelines* [CDDG]), one for primary care settings (*Diagnostic Descriptions for Primary Care*), and one for research purposes (*Diagnostic Descriptions for Research*). WHO understands that mental health clinicians, primary care physicians, and researchers differ in their coding needs for specificity. They also differ in the ways they think about the organization of disorders and differ in the first place they may typically search for a code within a system. When professionals are unable to locate a search object quickly, they are likely to abandon the search and consider the classification system an annoyance rather than a helpful tool. Therefore, the versions will have different content. For example, fewer disorders will be included in the primary care version, and the disorders are likely to have less descriptive information as well. The primary care version is intended for non-mental health specialty providers of care. Of course, psychologists or psychiatrists working in primary care settings would use the full ICD chapter for mental and behavioral disorders, not the shortened primary care version.

The elements of the revised ICD–11 CDDG will include the category name of a mental or behavioral condition, its definition, the essential features that are required to assign the category, the threshold boundary with normality, the boundary with other disorders (i.e., differential diagnosis), the coded qualifiers or subtypes, additional features relevant to the diagnosis, culture-related features, developmental presentations, and gender-related features (Reed, 2013).

It is important for clinicians to be aware that these updated CDDG for ICD–11 will be readily available. The WHO Department of Mental Health and Substance Abuse is working on this material at the same time as the overall classification. They plan to release the CDDG as a separate resource simultaneously with the release of the ICD–11 code set. In the event that the publication of ICD–11 is delayed for any reason, they may be able to release the field trials version of the CDDG in advance of ICD publication so that people in the field can start using it and preparing for ICD–11 rollout as quickly as possible (G. M. Reed, personal communication, May 18, 2013).

A Focus on Clinical Utility

To fulfill the major aims of the revision for ICD–11, multiple attempts to better classify diagnoses have been undertaken worldwide. Readers may refer to the section on clinical utility issues in Chapter 4 of this primer for background on the criticisms of current systems (ICD–10, *Diagnostic and Statistical Manual of Mental Disorders, Fourth Edition, Text Revision* [DSM–IV–TR, American Psychiatric Association, 2000], and DSM–5 [American Psychiatric Association, 2013a]) and their non–practice-friendly nature and forced hierarchies. Addressing the shortcomings of current taxonomies has been a WHO priority for the new revision from the outset. The WHO Department of Mental Health and Substance Abuse initiated a number of field studies to determine the best structure to enhance the clinical utility of ICD–11. Clinical utility is actually a key factor in decisions the department will make, with the input of its global experts, regarding what to include in the new revision. This is in sharp contrast to the lack of preassessment studies for DSM–5 to determine its clinical utility issues. To carry out their work, the department created a field studies coordination group for ICD–11 Mental and Behavioural Disorders and a network of formative field study centers across 10 countries, including the United States. The research includes global formative field studies, evaluative field studies, a global clinical practice network for Internet-based field studies, and clinic-based field studies.

Clinicians want to be able to find the diagnoses they need quickly and efficiently. Well aware of this, specialists at WHO working on the current revision see it as a substantial opportunity to improve the clinical usefulness of the system. The WHO Department of Mental Health and Substance Abuse has taken care to establish a comprehensive working definition for the clinical utility of a construct or diagnostic category in the system. The definition encompasses four principal aspects: (a) its communication value; (b) its implementation characteristics such as ease of use, accuracy, and feasibility; (c) its utility for choosing interventions and making clinical management decisions; and (d) the aspirational addition of improvements in clinical outcomes (Reed, 2010).

Evidence from neuroscience research and genetics research does not yet support major changes for the specific disorders or the specific classification structure (Reed, 2012). Thus, the essential differences that clinicians will notice in ICD–11 are related to its ease of use and goodness of fit in daily practice. In the end, the ways in which a diagnostic system is organized either hinder or contribute to clinical utility. Field studies show that ICD–11 taxonomy will better reflect how clinicians think about mental conditions, and that factor will be a marked improvement over ICD–10 and DSM–IV–TR (Roberts et al., 2012). DSM–5, however, is designed to be compatible with ICD–10–CM, although it also has to work with ICD–9–CM until October 2014, and it has to anticipate the revised categories of ICD–11. As a result of planning and research on feasibility and goodness of fit issues, ICD–11 is likely to be the more clinically useful of the two systems. This outcome is even more likely when ICD–11 is used with the accompanying updated version of the CDDG, because the package aligns mental and behavioral health professionals in the United States with the global community of clinicians.

Professionals' Natural Common Groupings of Mental Disorders

A classification system is a bridge between the patient's clinical presentation and the health care professional's mapping or conceptualization of the patient's condition. For the system to be useful to practitioners, it has to facilitate recognition of mental disorders and inform the ensuing treatment recommendations.

The evidence base that influences and supports the ICD–11 metastructure is strong. Of the many studies and journal articles related to ICD–11 published to date, the most striking finding (to this clinician author's mind) came from a field study that examined well-trained and experienced mental health professionals' conceptualizations of how mental disorders relate to each other (Reed et al., 2013). Guided by their clinical experience, 517 participants (73.3% psychiatrists, 24.8% psychologists, 1.9% other professionals such as psychiatric nurses and social workers) from eight countries (Brazil, China, India, Japan, Mexico, Nigeria, Spain, and the United States) sorted a set of cards containing the names of mental disorders into groups. They sorted the cards according to their perceptions of the disorders' similarities and the clinical management of the conditions; participants then formed a hierarchical structure, aggregating and disaggregating their groupings.

> This study revealed a "natural taxonomy" of mental disorders held by global mental health professionals that was stunningly consistent, with correlation coefficients higher than .90 across countries (Table 4), languages, classification system used (Table 5), and professional discipline. In the context of considerable discussion about the lack of reliability among clinicians (e.g., Garb, 2005; Regier et al., 2013), these results are quite striking. Clinicians interact with people with mental and behavioural disorders on a daily basis, and form implicit (or sometimes explicit) views of the relationships among disorders (Egli et al., 2006; Flanagan et al., 2008; Roberts et al., 2012). At the same time, clinicians' perspectives are obviously shaped by training and theoretical and practical knowledge about the nature of psychopathology, which is increasingly shared throughout the world. The ways in which the clinician-generated classification structure deviates from current classification systems are neither random nor idiosyncratic, but they are strongly shared across countries, languages, and the professional disciplines of psychiatry and psychology. (Reed et al., 2013, p. 18)

The natural taxonomy of clinicians was both rational and interpretable, and it formed a stable, robust, shared construction. The organization was different from those of ICD–10 and DSM–IV–TR but quite consistent with ICD–11 as it is being developed.

Reed and his 19 coauthors from around the globe (2013) were careful to note that clinicians' natural taxonomies should not take precedence over other forms of evidence. Scientific evidence should be used in the development of the classification structure where there is compelling and dispositive (i.e., conclusive) data. They suggest, however, that professionals' cognitive classification structures will help in identifying where notable differences, should there be any, may be addressed by targeted education efforts for the new ICD–11.

The results of the Reed et al. (2013) study were similar to those of a larger study that used completely different methods (Roberts et al., 2012). In that study, 1,371 psychiatrists and psychologists from 64 countries were surveyed via the Internet about the relationship among grouping structures for mental disorders. Participants rated similarities among mental disorders presented as paired comparisons. The surveyed clinicians by and large used three distinctive dimensions to make clinical categorization judgments: an internalizing versus externalizing trend, developmental versus adult onset, and functional versus organic syndromes. Results showed clinicians' conceptualizations were rational and stable across differing professions, languages, and countries' level of income. Roberts and his colleagues (2012) concluded that there is actually more concordance among global clinicians than there is among the classification systems currently in use. Further, if clinicians are expected to be able to find what they are seeking, their conceptual maps should be taken into account in designing new versions of classification systems based on how clinicians search within a classification system. The Roberts et al. study found that clinicians did not view obsessive–compulsive disorder and body dysmorphic disorder as similar, for example, although DSM–5 groups them together. However, the ICD–11 metastructure fits clinicians' conceptual mapping better than does ICD–10 or DSM–5.

In addition to the two taxonomy studies just described, there have been two important worldwide formative field trial surveys that are especially relevant to clinicians' professional needs. In the first, Reed, Correia, Esparza, Saxena, and Maj (2011) reported on the joint World Psychiatric Association (WPA)–WHO survey of 4,887 psychiatrists in 44 nations concerning their clinical use of diagnostic classification systems and the characteristics they wished to see in the classification of mental disorders. Findings from the study informed the ICD–11 developers that the great majority of psychiatrists wanted a simpler system with less than 100 categories, and two thirds of them wanted flexible guidance rather than a fixed set of criteria. Overall, most respondents were open to the inclusion of a dimensional component, whereas responses were more mixed about whether, or how best, to incorporate severity and functional status. Many of the psychiatrists in Latin America and Asia noted cross-cultural applicability problems within the current systems in use. Although respondents found ease of use and goodness of fit sufficiently high for most diagnostic categories in ICD–10, they also rated some specific categories low in clinical utility. By a large margin, the psychiatrists agreed that the primary aims of a classification system are to facilitate communication and inform clinical decision making.

The second formative study (Evans et al., 2013) was a WHO–IUPsyS multilingual survey investigating the perspectives of 2,155 psychologists in 23 countries on the diagnostic classification of mental disorders. The results were similar to those of the WPA–WHO survey: Psychologists also agreed that the primary purposes of a classification system are to facilitate communication and guide treatment decisions, and they favored flexible guidelines over fixed criteria. They too supported most diagnostic categories, and at the same time noted problematic specific diagnoses. A large percentage of psychologists outside the United States and Europe, in particular, reported both cross-cultural applicability problems and cultural bias. In sum, despite differences between the two studies in the profession of participants (psychiatrists and psychologists), the results were remarkably similar. Clinicians across professions viewed clinical utility as a priority for ICD–11, and they called for improvements in cross-cultural applicability.

As the studies for ICD–11 continue, two bodies are being used to advance the ICD–11 development: The Global Clinical Practice Network implements Internet-based methodologies and the International Field Studies Centers conducts the clinic-based field studies.

It should be heartening to mental health professionals everywhere to know that because of these kinds of scientific field study approaches, their clinical judgments and professional perspectives are being used to maximize clinical utility for ICD–11 without sacrificing scientific validity.

Proposed ICD–11 Structure for Mental and Behavioral Disorders

All the details of ICD–11 have not yet been finalized. However, major broad decisions have been made as the surveys and field studies have progressed and their findings have been taken into account for the new organizational structure (see Table 5.1). The mental and behavioral disorders chapter will have a greater number of diagnostic block divisions, resulting in a structure that is "flatter" and more clinically intuitive. There are more category blocks because the developers will not force disorders into a common grouping unless there is sufficient justification for doing so. The following are the anticipated 21 diagnostic blocks:

> ➤ Neurodevelopmental disorders
> ➤ Schizophrenia spectrum and other primary psychotic disorders
> ➤ Catatonia
> ➤ Bipolar and related disorders
> ➤ Depressive disorders
> ➤ Anxiety and fear-related disorders
> ➤ Obsessive–compulsive and related disorders
> ➤ Disorders specifically associated with stress
> ➤ Dissociative disorders
> ➤ Bodily distress disorders, and psychological and behavioral factors associated with disorders or diseases categorized elsewhere
> ➤ Feeding and eating disorders
> ➤ Elimination disorders
> ➤ Substance use disorders
> ➤ Substance-induced mental and behavioral disorders
> ➤ Impulse control disorders
> ➤ Disruptive behavior and dissocial disorders
> ➤ Disorders of personality
> ➤ Paraphilic disorders
> ➤ Factitious disorders
> ➤ Neurocognitive disorders
> ➤ Mental and behavioral disorders associated with disorders or diseases classified elsewhere

Two new proposed chapters in ICD–11 are relevant to psychologists as well as physicians. According to Reed (2012), the suggested new chapter on sleep disorders will incorporate the

TABLE 5.1
High-Level (Block) Proposed Linear Structure for ICD–11 Mental and Behavioral Disorders and Comparison With DSM–5

ICD–11>	DSM–5
NEURODEVELOPMENTAL DISORDERS	NEURODEVELOPMENTAL DISORDERS
SCHIZOPHRENIA SPECTRUM AND OTHER PRIMARY PSYCHOTIC DISORDERS	SCHIZOPHRENIA SPECTRUM AND OTHER PSYCHOTIC DISORDERS
CATATONIA	[Included in Schizophrenia Spectrum and Other Psychotic Disorders]
BIPOLAR AND RELATED DISORDERS	BIPOLAR AND RELATED DISORDERS
DEPRESSIVE DISORDERS	DEPRESSIVE DISORDERS
ANXIETY AND FEAR-RELATED DISORDERS	ANXIETY DISORDERS
OBSESSIVE–COMPULSIVE AND RELATED DISORDERS	OBSESSIVE–COMPULSIVE AND RELATED DISORDERS
DISORDERS SPECIFICALLY ASSOCIATED WITH STRESS	TRAUMA- AND STRESSOR-RELATED DISORDERS
DISSOCIATIVE DISORDERS	DISSOCIATIVE DISORDERS
BODILY DISTRESS DISORDERS, AND PSYCHOLOGICAL AND BEHAVIORAL FACTORS ASSOCIATED WITH DISORDERS OR DISEASES CLASSIFIED ELSEWHERE	SOMATIC SYMPTOM AND RELATED DISORDERS
FEEDING AND EATING DISORDERS	FEEDING AND EATING DISORDERS
ELIMINATION DISORDERS	ELIMINATION DISORDERS
[Separate chapter on Sleep–Wake Disorders]	SLEEP–WAKE DISORDERS
[To be incorporated into separate chapter on Sexuality-Related Conditions and Dysfunctions]	SEXUAL DYSFUNCTIONS

(*continued*)

TABLE 5.1 (*Continued*)
High-Level (Block) Proposed Linear Structure for ICD–11 Mental and Behavioral Disorders and Comparison With DSM–5

ICD–11>	DSM–5
[To be incorporated into separate chapter on Sexuality-Related Conditions and Dysfunctions]	GENDER DYSPHORIA
SUBSTANCE USE DISORDERS	SUBSTANCE-RELATED DISORDERS (Substantially different organization)
SUBSTANCE-INDUCED MENTAL AND BEHAVIORAL DISORDERS[a]	SUBSTANCE-INDUCED DISORDERS
IMPULSE CONTROL DISORDERS (includes Pathological Gambling; does not contain Internet Use Disorder)	DISRUPTIVE, IMPULSE-CONTROL, AND CONDUCT DISORDERS [Combined with Disruptive and Conduct Disorders; Gambling incorporated in DSM–5 in Non-Substance-Related Disorders; Internet Use Disorder in research appendix. Different order; appears before Substance-Related and Addictive Disorders]
DISRUPTIVE BEHAVIOR AND DISSOCIAL DISORDERS	DISRUPTIVE, IMPULSE-CONTROL, AND CONDUCT DISORDERS [Combined with Impulse Control Disorders; different order; appears before Substance-Related and Addictive Disorders]
DISORDERS OF PERSONALITY	PERSONALITY DISORDERS [Different order; appears after Neurocognitive Disorders]
PARAPHILIC DISORDERS	PARAPHILIC DISORDERS
FACTITIOUS DISORDERS	[Included under Somatic Symptom Disorders]

TABLE 5.1 (*Continued*)
High-Level (Block) Proposed Linear Structure for ICD–11 Mental and Behavioral Disorders and Comparison With DSM–5

ICD–11>	DSM–5
NEUROCOGNITIVE DISORDERS	NEUROCOGNITIVE DISORDERS (Different order; appears before Personality Disorders)
MENTAL AND BEHAVIORAL DISORDERS ASSOCIATED WITH DISORDERS OR DISEASES CLASSIFIED ELSEWHERE[b]	[DSM–5 divides these up into the section that corresponds to the expressed symptoms. For example, 'Depressive disorder associated with another medical condition' is listed under Depressive Disorders]
[Residual categories for each block will be available by default]	OTHER MENTAL DISORDERS
[In Diseases of the Nervous System, chapters on Substance-Related Disorders, or chapter on External Causes]	MEDICATION-INDUCED MOVEMENT DISORDERS AND OTHER ADVERSE EFFECTS OF MEDICATION
[Separate chapter on Factors Influencing Health Status and Encounters With Health Services]	OTHER CONDITIONS THAT MAY BE A FOCUS OF CLINICAL ATTENTION

Note. The information regarding ICD–11 in this table is based on current proposals of the ICD–11, which have not been approved by the World Health Assembly and therefore, do not represent the official policies of the World Health Organization. Geoffrey Reed (October 17, 2013).
[a]This block will be the primary parent of substance-induced mental and behavioral disorders, but they will also be cross-linked by secondary parenting to the block corresponding to the clinical manifestations of the conditions (e.g., Depressive disorders for Substance-induced depressive episodes). [b]These disorders may be instead grouped with equivalent symptom clusters (e.g., Depressive disorders for Depressive Disorder due to Disorder or Disease Classified Elsewhere). Need to consider best terminology. Also need to consider whether there is a need for additional puerperium-related disorders and if they fit here, or whether these are adequately covered by qualifiers in other sections.

"nonorganic" sleep disorders that are in the ICD–10 mental and behavioral disorders section, the "organic" sleep disorders from the section on diseases of the nervous system, and a few additional categories from other areas, such as sleep apnea from the respiratory diseases section. The new chapter on sexual health will incorporate "nonorganic" sexual dysfunctions from the mental and behavioral disorders section and "organic" sexual dysfunctions from the genitourinary section.

It is important to WHO that its classification system be useful to all clinicians who must be able to find the accurate diagnoses they need quickly, whether they are highly trained mental health professionals or service providers in primary care settings in developing nations with sparse training in mental disorders.

Implications for Clinical Care

To the extent that the promise of the forthcoming ICD–11 mental and behavioral disorders chapter is fulfilled, the WHO Department of Mental Health and Substance Abuse will offer a diagnostic system that facilitates clinicians' ability to identify treatment needs, deliver quality care, and reduce the burden of mental disorders globally. The more accurately ICD–11 describes mental health conditions as they present clinically and organizes the diagnoses into cohesive categories, the more likely it is that practitioners will find ICD–11 helpful and will actually use it well. Such an indicator of an enhanced level of clinical utility at the point of clinical contact can lead to better problem identification, treatment, and communication of vital health information.

The development of the ICD–11 chapter on mental and behavioral disorders has been a groundbreaking, transparent, multinational, multidisciplinary, multilingual scientific process in collaboration with stakeholders and independent of commercial influences. According to the information we possess now about ICD–11, the WHO resource is one to be welcomed as the next big step in helping practitioners better meet our patients' needs and further public health. Psychologists around the world, researchers and clinicians alike, can be proud of the outcome and appreciative of their opportunity to participate in improving the diagnostic system used by 194 nations.

ICD–10–CM Codes for Mental, Behavioral, and Neurodevelopmental Disorders

Mental, Behavioral, and Neurodevelopmental disorders (F01–F99)

Includes: disorders of psychological development

Excludes2: symptoms, signs and abnormal clinical laboratory findings, not elsewhere classified (R00–R99)

This chapter contains the following blocks:

F01–F09	Mental disorders due to known physiological conditions
F10–F19	Mental and behavioral disorders due to psychoactive substance use
F20–F29	Schizophrenia, schizotypal, delusional, and other non-mood psychotic disorders
F30–F39	Mood [affective] disorders
F40–F48	Anxiety, dissociative, stress-related, somatoform and other nonpsychotic mental disorders
F50–F59	Behavioral syndromes associated with physiological disturbances and physical factors

This appendix is from Chapter 5, "Mental, Behavioral, and Neurodevelopmental Disorders," of the 2014 *ICD–10–CM Tabular List of Diseases and Injuries*, developed by the Centers for Medicare and Medicaid Services with support from the Centers for Disease Control and Prevention, National Center for Health Statistics. Retrieved from http://www.cdc.gov/nchs/icd/icd10cm.htm#icd2014. In the public domain.

F60–F69 Disorders of adult personality and behavior

F70–F79 Intellectual disabilities

F80–F89 Pervasive and specific developmental disorders

F90–F98 Behavioral and emotional disorders with onset usually occurring in childhood and adolescence

F99 Unspecified mental disorder

Mental disorders due to known physiological conditions (F01–F09)

Note: This block comprises a range of mental disorders grouped together on the basis of their having in common a demonstrable etiology in cerebral disease, brain injury, or other insult leading to cerebral dysfunction. The dysfunction may be primary, as in diseases, injuries, and insults that affect the brain directly and selectively; or secondary, as in systemic diseases and disorders that attack the brain only as one of the multiple organs or systems of the body that are involved.

F01 Vascular dementia

Vascular dementia as a result of infarction of the brain due to vascular disease, including hypertensive cerebrovascular disease.

Includes: arteriosclerotic dementia

Code first the underlying physiological condition or sequelae of cerebrovascular disease.

F01.5 Vascular dementia

F01.50 Vascular dementia without behavioral disturbance

F01.51 Vascular dementia with behavioral disturbance

Vascular dementia with aggressive behavior
Vascular dementia with combative behavior
Vascular dementia with violent behavior

Use additional code, if applicable, to identify wandering in vascular dementia (Z91.83)

F02 Dementia in other diseases classified elsewhere

Code first the underlying physiological condition, such as:
Alzheimer's (G30.–)
cerebral lipidosis (E75.4)
Creutzfeldt-Jakob disease (A81.0–)
dementia with Lewy bodies (G31.83)
epilepsy and recurrent seizures (G40.–)
frontotemporal dementia (G31.09)
hepatolenticular degeneration (E83.0)
human immunodeficiency virus [HIV] disease (B20)
hypercalcemia (E83.52)
hypothyroidism, acquired (E00–E03.–)
intoxications (T36–T65)
Jakob-Creutzfeldt disease (A81.0–)
multiple sclerosis (G35)
neurosyphilis (A52.17)
niacin deficiency [pellagra] (E52)
Parkinson's disease (G20)
Pick's disease (G31.01)
polyarteritis nodosa (M30.0)
systemic lupus erythematosus (M32.–)
trypanosomiasis (B56.–, B57.–)
vitamin B deficiency (E53.8)

Excludes1: dementia with Parkinsonism (G31.83)

Excludes2: dementia in alcohol and psychoactive substance disorders (F10–F19, with .17, .27, .97)
vascular dementia (F01.5–)

F02.8 Dementia in other diseases classified elsewhere

F02.80 Dementia in other diseases classified elsewhere without behavioral disturbance
Dementia in other diseases classified elsewhere NOS

F02.81 Dementia in other diseases classified elsewhere with behavioral disturbance
Dementia in other diseases classified elsewhere with aggressive behavior

Dementia in other diseases classified elsewhere with combative behavior
Dementia in other diseases classified elsewhere with violent behavior

Use additional code, if applicable, to identify wandering in dementia in conditions classified elsewhere (Z91.83)

F03 Unspecified dementia

Presenile dementia NOS
Presenile psychosis NOS
Primary degenerative dementia NOS
Senile dementia NOS
Senile dementia depressed or paranoid type
Senile psychosis NOS

Excludes1: senility NOS (R41.81)

Excludes2: mild memory disturbance due to known physiological condition (F06.8)
senile dementia with delirium or acute confusional state (F05)

F03.9 Unspecified dementia

F03.90 Unspecified dementia without behavioral disturbance
Dementia NOS

F03.91 Unspecified dementia with behavioral disturbance
Unspecified dementia with aggressive behavior
Unspecified dementia with combative behavior
Unspecified dementia with violent behavior

Use additional code, if applicable, to identify wandering in unspecified dementia (Z91.83)

F04 Amnestic disorder due to known physiological condition

Korsakov's psychosis or syndrome, nonalcoholic

Code first the underlying physiological condition

Excludes1: amnesia NOS (R41.3)
anterograde amnesia (R41.1)
dissociative amnesia (F44.0)
retrograde amnesia (R41.2)

Excludes2: alcohol-induced or unspecified Korsakov's
syndrome (F10.26, F10.96)
Korsakov's syndrome induced by other psychoactive substances (F13.26, F13.96, F19.16,
F19.26, F19.96)

F05 Delirium due to known physiological condition

Acute or subacute brain syndrome
Acute or subacute confusional state (nonalcoholic)
Acute or subacute infective psychosis
Acute or subacute organic reaction
Acute or subacute psycho-organic syndrome
Delirium of mixed etiology
Delirium superimposed on dementia
Sundowning

Code first the underlying physiological condition

Excludes1: delirium NOS (R41.0)

Excludes2: delirium tremens alcohol-induced or unspecified
(F10.231, F10.921)

F06 Other mental disorders due to known physiological condition

Includes: mental disorders due to endocrine disorder
mental disorders due to exogenous hormone
mental disorders due to exogenous toxic substance
mental disorders due to primary cerebral disease
mental disorders due to somatic illness
mental disorders due to systemic disease affecting
the brain

Code first the underlying physiological condition

Excludes1: unspecified dementia (F03)

Excludes2: delirium due to known physiological
condition (F05)
dementia as classified in F01–F02
other mental disorders associated with alcohol
and other psychoactive substances (F10–F19)

F06.0 Psychotic disorder with hallucinations due to known physiological condition

Organic hallucinatory state (nonalcoholic)

Excludes2: hallucinations and perceptual disturbance induced by alcohol and other
psychoactive substances
(F10–F19 with .151, .251, .951)
schizophrenia (F20.–)

F06.1 Catatonic disorder due to known physiological condition

Excludes1: catatonic stupor (R40.1)
stupor NOS (R40.1)

Excludes2: catatonic schizophrenia (F20.2)
dissociative stupor (F44.2)

F06.2 Psychotic disorder with delusions due to known physiological condition

Paranoid and paranoid-hallucinatory organic states
Schizophrenia-like psychosis in epilepsy

Excludes2: alcohol and drug-induced psychotic
disorder (F10–F19 with .150, .250, .950)
brief psychotic disorder (F23)
delusional disorder (F22)
schizophrenia (F20.–)

F06.3 Mood disorder due to known physiological condition

Excludes2: mood disorders due to alcohol and
other psychoactive substances (F10–F19
with .14, .24, .94)
mood disorders, not due to known
physiological condition or unspecified
(F30–F39)

**F06.30 Mood disorder due to known physiologi-
cal condition, unspecified**

**F06.31 Mood disorder due to known physiological
condition with depressive features**

F06.32 Mood disorder due to known physiological condition with major depressive-like episode

F06.33 Mood disorder due to known physiological condition with manic features

F06.34 Mood disorder due to known physiological condition with mixed features

F06.4 Anxiety disorder due to known physiological condition

> **Excludes2:** anxiety disorders due to alcohol and other psychoactive substances (F10–F19 with .180, .280, .980)
> anxiety disorders, not due to known physiological condition or unspecified (F40.–, F41.–)

F06.8 Other specified mental disorders due to known physiological condition

Epileptic psychosis NOS
Organic dissociative disorder
Organic emotionally labile [asthenic] disorder

F07 Personality and behavioral disorders due to known physiological condition

Code first the underlying physiological condition

F07.0 Personality change due to known physiological condition

Frontal lobe syndrome
Limbic epilepsy personality syndrome
Lobotomy syndrome
Organic personality disorder
Organic pseudopsychopathic personality
Organic pseudoretarded personality
Postleucotomy syndrome

Code first underlying physiological condition

Excludes1: mild cognitive impairment (G31.84)
postconcussional syndrome (F07.81)

postencephalitic syndrome (F07.89)
signs and symptoms involving emotional
state (R45.–)

Excludes2: specific personality disorder (F60.–)

F07.8 Other personality and behavioral disorders due to known physiological condition

F07.81 Postconcussional syndrome

Postcontusional syndrome (encephalopathy)
Post-traumatic brain syndrome, nonpsychotic

Use additional code to identify associated
post-traumatic headache, if applicable
(G44.3–)

Excludes1: current concussion (brain) (S06.0–)
postencephalitic syndrome
(F07.89)

F07.89 Other personality and behavioral disorders due to known physiological condition

Postencephalitic syndrome
Right hemispheric organic affective disorder

F07.9 Unspecified personality and behavioral disorder due to known physiological condition

Organic psychosyndrome

F09 Unspecified mental disorder due to known physiological condition

Mental disorder NOS due to known physiological condition
Organic brain syndrome NOS
Organic mental disorder NOS
Organic psychosis NOS
Symptomatic psychosis NOS

Code first the underlying physiological condition

Excludes1: psychosis NOS (F29)

Mental and behavioral disorders due to psychoactive substance use (F10–F19)

F10 Alcohol related disorders

Use additional code for blood alcohol level, if applicable
(Y90.–)

F10.1 **Alcohol abuse**

> **Excludes1:** alcohol dependence (F10.2–)
> alcohol use, unspecified (F10.9–)

F10.10 **Alcohol abuse, uncomplicated**

F10.12 **Alcohol abuse with intoxication**

> F10.120 **Alcohol abuse with intoxication, uncomplicated**
>
> F10.121 **Alcohol abuse with intoxication delirium**
>
> F10.129 **Alcohol abuse with intoxication, unspecified**

F10.14 **Alcohol abuse with alcohol-induced mood disorder**

F10.15 **Alcohol abuse with alcohol-induced psychotic disorder**

> F10.150 **Alcohol abuse with alcohol-induced psychotic disorder with delusions**
>
> F10.151 **Alcohol abuse with alcohol-induced psychotic disorder with hallucinations**
>
> F10.159 **Alcohol abuse with alcohol-induced psychotic disorder, unspecified**

F10.18 **Alcohol abuse with other alcohol-induced disorders**

> F10.180 **Alcohol abuse with alcohol-induced anxiety disorder**
>
> F10.181 **Alcohol abuse with alcohol-induced sexual dysfunction**
>
> F10.182 **Alcohol abuse with alcohol-induced sleep disorder**
>
> F10.188 **Alcohol abuse with other alcohol-induced disorder**

F10.19 **Alcohol abuse with unspecified alcohol-induced disorder**

F10.2 Alcohol dependence

> **Excludes1:** alcohol abuse (F10.1–)
>> alcohol use, unspecified (F10.9–)

> **Excludes2:** toxic effect of alcohol (T51.0–)

F10.20 Alcohol dependence, uncomplicated

F10.21 Alcohol dependence, in remission

F10.22 Alcohol dependence with intoxication

> Acute drunkenness (in alcoholism)

> **Excludes1:** alcohol dependence with withdrawal (F10.23–)

> **F10.220 Alcohol dependence with intoxication, uncomplicated**

> **F10.221 Alcohol dependence with intoxication delirium**

> **F10.229 Alcohol dependence with intoxication, unspecified**

F10.23 Alcohol dependence with withdrawal

> **Excludes1:** Alcohol dependence with intoxication (F10.22–)

> **F10.230 Alcohol dependence with withdrawal, uncomplicated**

> **F10.231 Alcohol dependence with withdrawal delirium**

> **F10.232 Alcohol dependence with withdrawal with perceptual disturbance**

> **F10.239 Alcohol dependence with withdrawal, unspecified**

F10.24 Alcohol dependence with alcohol-induced mood disorder

F10.25 Alcohol dependence with alcohol-induced psychotic disorder

> **F10.250 Alcohol dependence with alcohol-induced psychotic disorder with delusions**

F10.251   Alcohol dependence with alcohol-induced psychotic disorder with hallucinations

F10.259   Alcohol dependence with alcohol-induced psychotic disorder, unspecified

F10.26   Alcohol dependence with alcohol-induced persisting amnestic disorder

F10.27   Alcohol dependence with alcohol-induced persisting dementia

F10.28   Alcohol dependence with other alcohol-induced disorders

F10.280   Alcohol dependence with alcohol-induced anxiety disorder

F10.281   Alcohol dependence with alcohol-induced sexual dysfunction

F10.282   Alcohol dependence with alcohol-induced sleep disorder

F10.288   Alcohol dependence with other alcohol-induced disorder

F10.29   Alcohol dependence with unspecified alcohol-induced disorder

F10.9   Alcohol use, unspecified

Excludes1: alcohol abuse (F10.1–)
alcohol dependence (F10.2–)

F10.92   Alcohol use, unspecified with intoxication

F10.920   Alcohol use, unspecified with intoxication, uncomplicated

F10.921   Alcohol use, unspecified with intoxication delirium

F10.929   Alcohol use, unspecified with intoxication, unspecified

F10.94   Alcohol use, unspecified with alcohol-induced mood disorder

F10.95 Alcohol use, unspecified with alcohol-induced psychotic disorder

    F10.950 Alcohol use, unspecified with alcohol-induced psychotic disorder with delusions

    F10.951 Alcohol use, unspecified with alcohol-induced psychotic disorder with hallucinations

    F10.959 Alcohol use, unspecified with alcohol-induced psychotic disorder, unspecified

F10.96 Alcohol use, unspecified with alcohol-induced persisting amnestic disorder

F10.97 Alcohol use, unspecified with alcohol-induced persisting dementia

F10.98 Alcohol use, unspecified with other alcohol-induced disorders

    F10.980 Alcohol use, unspecified with alcohol-induced anxiety disorder

    F10.981 Alcohol use, unspecified with alcohol-induced sexual dysfunction

    F10.982 Alcohol use, unspecified with alcohol-induced sleep disorder

    F10.988 Alcohol use, unspecified with other alcohol-induced disorder

F10.99 Alcohol use, unspecified with unspecified alcohol-induced disorder

F11 Opioid related disorders

  F11.1 Opioid abuse

    Excludes1: opioid dependence (F11.2–)
             opioid use, unspecified (F11.9–)

  F11.10 Opioid abuse, uncomplicated

  F11.12 Opioid abuse with intoxication

    F11.120 Opioid abuse with intoxication, uncomplicated

F11.121 Opioid abuse with intoxication delirium

F11.122 Opioid abuse with intoxication with perceptual disturbance

F11.129 Opioid abuse with intoxication, unspecified

F11.14 Opioid abuse with opioid-induced mood disorder

F11.15 Opioid abuse with opioid-induced psychotic disorder

F11.150 Opioid abuse with opioid-induced psychotic disorder with delusions

F11.151 Opioid abuse with opioid-induced psychotic disorder with hallucinations

F11.159 Opioid abuse with opioid-induced psychotic disorder, unspecified

F11.18 Opioid abuse with other opioid-induced disorder

F11.181 Opioid abuse with opioid-induced sexual dysfunction

F11.182 Opioid abuse with opioid-induced sleep disorder

F11.188 Opioid abuse with other opioid-induced disorder

F11.19 Opioid abuse with unspecified opioid-induced disorder

F11.2 Opioid dependence

Excludes1: opioid abuse (F11.1–)
            opioid use, unspecified (F11.9–)

Excludes2: opioid poisoning (T40.0–T40.2–)

F11.20 Opioid dependence, uncomplicated

F11.21 Opioid dependence, in remission

F11.22 Opioid dependence with intoxication

Excludes1: opioid dependence with withdrawal (F11.23)

F11.220 Opioid dependence with intoxication, uncomplicated

F11.221 Opioid dependence with intoxication delirium

F11.222 Opioid dependence with intoxication with perceptual disturbance

F11.229 Opioid dependence with intoxication, unspecified

F11.23 Opioid dependence with withdrawal

Excludes1: opioid dependence with intoxication (F11.22–)

F11.24 Opioid dependence with opioid-induced mood disorder

F11.25 Opioid dependence with opioid-induced psychotic disorder

F11.250 Opioid dependence with opioid-induced psychotic disorder with delusions

F11.251 Opioid dependence with opioid-induced psychotic disorder with hallucinations

F11.259 Opioid dependence with opioid-induced psychotic disorder, unspecified

F11.28 Opioid dependence with other opioid-induced disorder

F11.281 Opioid dependence with opioid-induced sexual dysfunction

F11.282 Opioid dependence with opioid-induced sleep disorder

F11.288 Opioid dependence with other opioid-induced disorder

F11.29 Opioid dependence with unspecified opioid-induced disorder

F11.9 **Opioid use, unspecified**

Excludes1: opioid abuse (F11.1–)
opioid dependence (F11.2–)

F11.90 **Opioid use, unspecified, uncomplicated**

F11.92 **Opioid use, unspecified with intoxication**

Excludes1: opioid use, unspecified with withdrawal (F11.93)

F11.920 **Opioid use, unspecified with intoxication, uncomplicated**

F11.921 **Opioid use, unspecified with intoxication delirium**

F11.922 **Opioid use, unspecified with intoxication with perceptual disturbance**

F11.929 **Opioid use, unspecified with intoxication, unspecified**

F11.93 **Opioid use, unspecified with withdrawal**

Excludes1: opioid use, unspecified with intoxication (F11.92–)

F11.94 **Opioid use, unspecified with opioid-induced mood disorder**

F11.95 **Opioid use, unspecified with opioid-induced psychotic disorder**

F11.950 **Opioid use, unspecified with opioid-induced psychotic disorder with delusions**

F11.951 **Opioid use, unspecified with opioid-induced psychotic disorder with hallucinations**

F11.959 **Opioid use, unspecified with opioid-induced psychotic disorder, unspecified**

F11.98 **Opioid use, unspecified with other specified opioid-induced disorder**

F11.981 **Opioid use, unspecified with opioid-induced sexual dysfunction**

F11.982 Opioid use, unspecified with opioid-induced sleep disorder

F11.988 Opioid use, unspecified with other opioid-induced disorder

F11.99 Opioid use, unspecified with unspecified opioid-induced disorder

F12 Cannabis related disorders

Includes: marijuana

F12.1 Cannabis abuse

Excludes1: cannabis dependence (F12.2–)
cannabis use, unspecified (F12.9–)

F12.10 Cannabis abuse, uncomplicated

F12.12 Cannabis abuse with intoxication

F12.120 Cannabis abuse with intoxication, uncomplicated

F12.121 Cannabis abuse with intoxication delirium

F12.122 Cannabis abuse with intoxication with perceptual disturbance

F12.129 Cannabis abuse with intoxication, unspecified

F12.15 Cannabis abuse with psychotic disorder

F12.150 Cannabis abuse with psychotic disorder with delusions

F12.151 Cannabis abuse with psychotic disorder with hallucinations

F12.159 Cannabis abuse with psychotic disorder, unspecified

F12.18 Cannabis abuse with other cannabis-induced disorder

F12.180 Cannabis abuse with cannabis-induced anxiety disorder

F12.188 Cannabis abuse with other cannabis-induced disorder

F12.19 Cannabis abuse with unspecified cannabis-induced disorder

F12.2 Cannabis dependence

> Excludes1: cannabis abuse (F12.1–)
> cannabis use, unspecified (F12.9–)
>
> Excludes2: cannabis poisoning (T40.7–)
>
> F12.20 Cannabis dependence, uncomplicated
>
> F12.21 Cannabis dependence, in remission
>
> F12.22 Cannabis dependence with intoxication
>
> > F12.220 Cannabis dependence with intoxication, uncomplicated
> >
> > F12.221 Cannabis dependence with intoxication delirium
> >
> > F12.222 Cannabis dependence with intoxication with perceptual disturbance
> >
> > F12.229 Cannabis dependence with intoxication, unspecified
>
> F12.25 Cannabis dependence with psychotic disorder
>
> > F12.250 Cannabis dependence with psychotic disorder with delusions
> >
> > F12.251 Cannabis dependence with psychotic disorder with hallucinations
> >
> > F12.259 Cannabis dependence with psychotic disorder, unspecified
>
> F12.28 Cannabis dependence with other cannabis-induced disorder
>
> > F12.280 Cannabis dependence with cannabis-induced anxiety disorder
> >
> > F12.288 Cannabis dependence with other cannabis-induced disorder
>
> F12.29 Cannabis dependence with unspecified cannabis-induced disorder

F12.9 Cannabis use, unspecified

Excludes1: cannabis abuse (F12.1–)
cannabis dependence (F12.2–)

F12.90 Cannabis use, unspecified, uncomplicated

F12.92 Cannabis use, unspecified with intoxication

F12.920 Cannabis use, unspecified with intoxication, uncomplicated

F12.921 Cannabis use, unspecified with intoxication delirium

F12.922 Cannabis use, unspecified with intoxication with perceptual disturbance

F12.929 Cannabis use, unspecified with intoxication, unspecified

F12.95 Cannabis use, unspecified with psychotic disorder

F12.950 Cannabis use, unspecified with psychotic disorder with delusions

F12.951 Cannabis use, unspecified with psychotic disorder with hallucinations

F12.959 Cannabis use, unspecified with psychotic disorder, unspecified

F12.98 Cannabis use, unspecified with other cannabis-induced disorder

F12.980 Cannabis use, unspecified with anxiety disorder

F12.988 Cannabis use, unspecified with other cannabis-induced disorder

F12.99 Cannabis use, unspecified with unspecified cannabis-induced disorder

F13 Sedative, hypnotic, or anxiolytic related disorders

F13.1 Sedative, hypnotic or anxiolytic-related abuse

Excludes1: sedative, hypnotic or anxiolytic-related dependence (F13.2–)
sedative, hypnotic, or anxiolytic use, unspecified (F13.9–)

F13.10 Sedative, hypnotic or anxiolytic abuse, uncomplicated

F13.12 Sedative, hypnotic or anxiolytic abuse with intoxication

   F13.120 Sedative, hypnotic or anxiolytic abuse with intoxication, uncomplicated

   F13.121 Sedative, hypnotic or anxiolytic abuse with intoxication delirium

   F13.129 Sedative, hypnotic or anxiolytic abuse with intoxication, unspecified

F13.14 Sedative, hypnotic or anxiolytic abuse with sedative, hypnotic or anxiolytic-induced mood disorder

F13.15 Sedative, hypnotic or anxiolytic abuse with sedative, hypnotic or anxiolytic-induced psychotic disorder

   F13.150 Sedative, hypnotic or anxiolytic abuse with sedative, hypnotic or anxiolytic-induced psychotic disorder with delusions

   F13.151 Sedative, hypnotic or anxiolytic abuse with sedative, hypnotic or anxiolytic-induced psychotic disorder with hallucinations

   F13.159 Sedative, hypnotic or anxiolytic abuse with sedative, hypnotic or anxiolytic-induced psychotic disorder, unspecified

F13.18 Sedative, hypnotic or anxiolytic abuse with other sedative, hypnotic or anxiolytic-induced disorders

   F13.180 Sedative, hypnotic or anxiolytic abuse with sedative, hypnotic or anxiolytic-induced anxiety disorder

F13.181 Sedative, hypnotic or anxiolytic abuse with sedative, hypnotic or anxiolytic-induced sexual dysfunction

F13.182 Sedative, hypnotic or anxiolytic abuse with sedative, hypnotic or anxiolytic-induced sleep disorder

F13.188 Sedative, hypnotic or anxiolytic abuse with other sedative, hypnotic or anxiolytic-induced disorder

F13.19 Sedative, hypnotic or anxiolytic abuse with unspecified sedative, hypnotic or anxiolytic-induced disorder

F13.2 Sedative, hypnotic or anxiolytic-related dependence

Excludes1: sedative, hypnotic or anxiolytic-related abuse (F13.1–)
sedative, hypnotic, or anxiolytic use, unspecified (F13.9–)

Excludes2: sedative, hypnotic, or anxiolytic poisoning (T42.–)

F13.20 Sedative, hypnotic or anxiolytic dependence, uncomplicated

F13.21 Sedative, hypnotic or anxiolytic dependence, in remission

F13.22 Sedative, hypnotic or anxiolytic dependence with intoxication

Excludes1: sedative, hypnotic or anxiolytic dependence with withdrawal (F13.23–)

F13.220 Sedative, hypnotic or anxiolytic dependence with intoxication, uncomplicated

F13.221 Sedative, hypnotic or anxiolytic dependence with intoxication delirium

F13.229 Sedative, hypnotic or anxiolytic dependence with intoxication, unspecified

F13.23 Sedative, hypnotic or anxiolytic dependence with withdrawal

Excludes1: sedative, hypnotic or anxiolytic dependence with intoxication (F13.22–)

F13.230 Sedative, hypnotic or anxiolytic dependence with withdrawal, uncomplicated

F13.231 Sedative, hypnotic or anxiolytic dependence with withdrawal delirium

F13.232 Sedative, hypnotic or anxiolytic dependence with withdrawal with perceptual disturbance

F13.239 Sedative, hypnotic or anxiolytic dependence with withdrawal, unspecified

F13.24 Sedative, hypnotic or anxiolytic dependence with sedative, hypnotic or anxiolytic-induced mood disorder

F13.25 Sedative, hypnotic or anxiolytic dependence with sedative, hypnotic or anxiolytic-induced psychotic disorder

F13.250 Sedative, hypnotic or anxiolytic dependence with sedative, hypnotic or anxiolytic-induced psychotic disorder with delusions

F13.251 Sedative, hypnotic or anxiolytic dependence with sedative, hypnotic or anxiolytic-induced psychotic disorder with hallucinations

F13.259 Sedative, hypnotic or anxiolytic dependence with sedative, hypnotic or anxiolytic-induced psychotic disorder, unspecified

F13.26 Sedative, hypnotic or anxiolytic dependence with sedative, hypnotic or anxiolytic-induced persisting amnestic disorder

F13.27 Sedative, hypnotic or anxiolytic dependence with sedative, hypnotic or anxiolytic-induced persisting dementia

F13.28 Sedative, hypnotic or anxiolytic dependence with other sedative, hypnotic or anxiolytic-induced disorders

F13.280 Sedative, hypnotic or anxiolytic dependence with sedative, hypnotic or anxiolytic-induced anxiety disorder

F13.281 Sedative, hypnotic or anxiolytic dependence with sedative, hypnotic or anxiolytic-induced sexual dysfunction

F13.282 Sedative, hypnotic or anxiolytic dependence with sedative, hypnotic or anxiolytic-induced sleep disorder

F13.288 Sedative, hypnotic or anxiolytic dependence with other sedative, hypnotic or anxiolytic-induced disorder

F13.29 Sedative, hypnotic or anxiolytic dependence with unspecified sedative, hypnotic or anxiolytic-induced disorder

F13.9 Sedative, hypnotic or anxiolytic-related use, unspecified

Excludes1: sedative, hypnotic or anxiolytic-related abuse (F13.1–)
sedative, hypnotic or anxiolytic-related dependence (F13.2–)

F13.90 Sedative, hypnotic, or anxiolytic use, unspecified, uncomplicated

F13.92 Sedative, hypnotic or anxiolytic use, unspecified with intoxication

> Excludes1: sedative, hypnotic or anxiolytic use, unspecified with withdrawal (F13.93–)

> F13.920 Sedative, hypnotic or anxiolytic use, unspecified with intoxication, uncomplicated

> F13.921 Sedative, hypnotic or anxiolytic use, unspecified with intoxication delirium

> F13.929 Sedative, hypnotic or anxiolytic use, unspecified with intoxication, unspecified

F13.93 Sedative, hypnotic or anxiolytic use, unspecified with withdrawal

> Excludes1: sedative, hypnotic or anxiolytic use, unspecified with intoxication (F13.92–)

> F13.930 Sedative, hypnotic or anxiolytic use, unspecified with withdrawal, uncomplicated

> F13.931 Sedative, hypnotic or anxiolytic use, unspecified with withdrawal delirium

> F13.932 Sedative, hypnotic or anxiolytic use, unspecified with withdrawal with perceptual disturbances

> F13.939 Sedative, hypnotic or anxiolytic use, unspecified with withdrawal, unspecified

F13.94 Sedative, hypnotic or anxiolytic use, unspecified with sedative, hypnotic or anxiolytic-induced mood disorder

F13.95 Sedative, hypnotic or anxiolytic use, unspecified with sedative, hypnotic or anxiolytic-induced psychotic disorder

F13.950 Sedative, hypnotic or anxiolytic use, unspecified with sedative, hypnotic or anxiolytic-induced psychotic disorder with delusions

F13.951 Sedative, hypnotic or anxiolytic use, unspecified with sedative, hypnotic or anxiolytic-induced psychotic disorder with hallucinations

F13.959 Sedative, hypnotic or anxiolytic use, unspecified with sedative, hypnotic or anxiolytic-induced psychotic disorder, unspecified

F13.96 Sedative, hypnotic or anxiolytic use, unspecified with sedative, hypnotic or anxiolytic-induced persisting amnestic disorder

F13.97 Sedative, hypnotic or anxiolytic use, unspecified with sedative, hypnotic or anxiolytic-induced persisting dementia

F13.98 Sedative, hypnotic or anxiolytic use, unspecified with other sedative, hypnotic or anxiolytic-induced disorders

F13.980 Sedative, hypnotic or anxiolytic use, unspecified with sedative, hypnotic or anxiolytic-induced anxiety disorder

F13.981 Sedative, hypnotic or anxiolytic use, unspecified with sedative, hypnotic or anxiolytic-induced sexual dysfunction

F13.982 Sedative, hypnotic or anxiolytic use, unspecified with sedative, hypnotic or anxiolytic-induced sleep disorder

F13.988 Sedative, hypnotic or anxiolytic use, unspecified with other sedative, hypnotic or anxiolytic-induced disorder

F13.99 Sedative, hypnotic or anxiolytic use, unspecified with unspecified sedative, hypnotic or anxiolytic-induced disorder

F14 Cocaine related disorders

Excludes2: other stimulant-related disorders (F15.–)

F14.1 Cocaine abuse

Excludes1: cocaine dependence (F14.2–)
cocaine use, unspecified (F14.9–)

F14.10 Cocaine abuse, uncomplicated

F14.12 Cocaine abuse with intoxication

F14.120 Cocaine abuse with intoxication, uncomplicated

F14.121 Cocaine abuse with intoxication with delirium

F14.122 Cocaine abuse with intoxication with perceptual disturbance

F14.129 Cocaine abuse with intoxication, unspecified

F14.14 Cocaine abuse with cocaine-induced mood disorder

F14.15 Cocaine abuse with cocaine-induced psychotic disorder

F14.150 Cocaine abuse with cocaine-induced psychotic disorder with delusions

F14.151 Cocaine abuse with cocaine-induced psychotic disorder with hallucinations

F14.159 Cocaine abuse with cocaine-induced psychotic disorder, unspecified

F14.18 Cocaine abuse with other cocaine-induced disorder

    F14.180 Cocaine abuse with cocaine-induced anxiety disorder

    F14.181 Cocaine abuse with cocaine-induced sexual dysfunction

    F14.182 Cocaine abuse with cocaine-induced sleep disorder

    F14.188 Cocaine abuse with other cocaine-induced disorder

F14.19 Cocaine abuse with unspecified cocaine-induced disorder

F14.2 Cocaine dependence

Excludes1: cocaine abuse (F14.1–)
cocaine use, unspecified (F14.9–)

Excludes2: cocaine poisoning (T40.5–)

F14.20 Cocaine dependence, uncomplicated

F14.21 Cocaine dependence, in remission

F14.22 Cocaine dependence with intoxication

Excludes1: cocaine dependence with withdrawal (F14.23)

    F14.220 Cocaine dependence with intoxication, uncomplicated

    F14.221 Cocaine dependence with intoxication delirium

    F14.222 Cocaine dependence with intoxication with perceptual disturbance

    F14.229 Cocaine dependence with intoxication, unspecified

F14.23 Cocaine dependence with withdrawal

Excludes1: cocaine dependence with intoxication (F14.22–)

F14.24 Cocaine dependence with cocaine-induced mood disorder

F14.25 Cocaine dependence with cocaine-induced psychotic disorder

    F14.250 Cocaine dependence with cocaine-induced psychotic disorder with delusions

    F14.251 Cocaine dependence with cocaine-induced psychotic disorder with hallucinations

    F14.259 Cocaine dependence with cocaine-induced psychotic disorder, unspecified

F14.28 Cocaine dependence with other cocaine-induced disorder

    F14.280 Cocaine dependence with cocaine-induced anxiety disorder

    F14.281 Cocaine dependence with cocaine-induced sexual dysfunction

    F14.282 Cocaine dependence with cocaine-induced sleep disorder

    F14.288 Cocaine dependence with other cocaine-induced disorder

F14.29 Cocaine dependence with unspecified cocaine-induced disorder

F14.9 Cocaine use, unspecified

Excludes1: cocaine abuse (F14.1–)
                cocaine dependence (F14.2–)

F14.90 Cocaine use, unspecified, uncomplicated

F14.92 Cocaine use, unspecified with intoxication

    F14.920 Cocaine use, unspecified with intoxication, uncomplicated

    F14.921 Cocaine use, unspecified with intoxication delirium

    F14.922 Cocaine use, unspecified with intoxication with perceptual disturbance

    F14.929 Cocaine use, unspecified with intoxication, unspecified

F14.94 Cocaine use, unspecified with cocaine-induced mood disorder

F14.95 Cocaine use, unspecified with cocaine-induced psychotic disorder

> F14.950 Cocaine use, unspecified with cocaine-induced psychotic disorder with delusions

> F14.951 Cocaine use, unspecified with cocaine-induced psychotic disorder with hallucinations

> F14.959 Cocaine use, unspecified with cocaine-induced psychotic disorder, unspecified

F14.98 Cocaine use, unspecified with other specified cocaine-induced disorder

> F14.980 Cocaine use, unspecified with cocaine-induced anxiety disorder

> F14.981 Cocaine use, unspecified with cocaine-induced sexual dysfunction

> F14.982 Cocaine use, unspecified with cocaine-induced sleep disorder

> F14.988 Cocaine use, unspecified with other cocaine-induced disorder

F14.99 Cocaine use, unspecified with unspecified cocaine-induced disorder

F15 Other stimulant related disorders

Includes: amphetamine-related disorders
caffeine

Excludes2: cocaine-related disorders (F14.–)

F15.1 Other stimulant abuse

Excludes1: other stimulant dependence (F15.2–)
other stimulant use, unspecified (F15.9–)

F15.10 Other stimulant abuse, uncomplicated

F15.12 Other stimulant abuse with intoxication

  F15.120 Other stimulant abuse with intoxication, uncomplicated

  F15.121 Other stimulant abuse with intoxication delirium

  F15.122 Other stimulant abuse with intoxication with perceptual disturbance

  F15.129 Other stimulant abuse with intoxication, unspecified

F15.14 Other stimulant abuse with stimulant-induced mood disorder

F15.15 Other stimulant abuse with stimulant-induced psychotic disorder

  F15.150 Other stimulant abuse with stimulant-induced psychotic disorder with delusions

  F15.151 Other stimulant abuse with stimulant-induced psychotic disorder with hallucinations

  F15.159 Other stimulant abuse with stimulant-induced psychotic disorder, unspecified

F15.18 Other stimulant abuse with other stimulant-induced disorder

  F15.180 Other stimulant abuse with stimulant-induced anxiety disorder

  F15.181 Other stimulant abuse with stimulant-induced sexual dysfunction

  F15.182 Other stimulant abuse with stimulant-induced sleep disorder

  F15.188 Other stimulant abuse with other stimulant-induced disorder

F15.19 Other stimulant abuse with unspecified stimulant-induced disorder

F15.2 **Other stimulant dependence**

Excludes1: other stimulant abuse (F15.1–)
other stimulant use, unspecified (F15.9–)

F15.20 **Other stimulant dependence, uncomplicated**

F15.21 **Other stimulant dependence, in remission**

F15.22 **Other stimulant dependence with intoxication**

Excludes1: other stimulant dependence with withdrawal (F15.23)

F15.220 **Other stimulant dependence with intoxication, uncomplicated**

F15.221 **Other stimulant dependence with intoxication delirium**

F15.222 **Other stimulant dependence with intoxication with perceptual disturbance**

F15.229 **Other stimulant dependence with intoxication, unspecified**

F15.23 **Other stimulant dependence with withdrawal**

Excludes1: other stimulant dependence with intoxication (F15.22–)

F15.24 **Other stimulant dependence with stimulant-induced mood disorder**

F15.25 **Other stimulant dependence with stimulant-induced psychotic disorder**

F15.250 **Other stimulant dependence with stimulant-induced psychotic disorder with delusions**

F15.251 **Other stimulant dependence with stimulant-induced psychotic disorder with hallucinations**

F15.259 **Other stimulant dependence with stimulant-induced psychotic disorder, unspecified**

F15.28 Other stimulant dependence with other stimulant-induced disorder

>> F15.280 Other stimulant dependence with stimulant-induced anxiety disorder

>> F15.281 Other stimulant dependence with stimulant-induced sexual dysfunction

>> F15.282 Other stimulant dependence with stimulant-induced sleep disorder

>> F15.288 Other stimulant dependence with other stimulant-induced disorder

F15.29 Other stimulant dependence with unspecified stimulant-induced disorder

F15.9 Other stimulant use, unspecified

> Excludes1: other stimulant abuse (F15.1–)
> other stimulant dependence (F15.2–)

F15.90 Other stimulant use, unspecified, uncomplicated

F15.92 Other stimulant use, unspecified with intoxication

> Excludes1: other stimulant use, unspecified with withdrawal (F15.93)

>> F15.920 Other stimulant use, unspecified with intoxication, uncomplicated

>> F15.921 Other stimulant use, unspecified with intoxication delirium

>> F15.922 Other stimulant use, unspecified with intoxication with perceptual disturbance

>> F15.929 Other stimulant use, unspecified with intoxication, unspecified

F15.93 Other stimulant use, unspecified with withdrawal

> Excludes1: other stimulant use, unspecified with intoxication (F15.92–)

F15.94   Other stimulant use, unspecified with stimulant-induced mood disorder

F15.95   Other stimulant use, unspecified with stimulant-induced psychotic disorder

> **F15.950   Other stimulant use, unspecified with stimulant-induced psychotic disorder with delusions**
>
> **F15.951   Other stimulant use, unspecified with stimulant-induced psychotic disorder with hallucinations**
>
> **F15.959   Other stimulant use, unspecified with stimulant-induced psychotic disorder, unspecified**

F15.98   Other stimulant use, unspecified with other stimulant-induced disorder

> **F15.980   Other stimulant use, unspecified with stimulant-induced anxiety disorder**
>
> **F15.981   Other stimulant use, unspecified with stimulant-induced sexual dysfunction**
>
> **F15.982   Other stimulant use, unspecified with stimulant-induced sleep disorder**
>
> **F15.988   Other stimulant use, unspecified with other stimulant-induced disorder**

F15.99   Other stimulant use, unspecified with unspecified stimulant-induced disorder

F16   Hallucinogen related disorders

Includes: ecstasy
PCP
phencyclidine

F16.1   Hallucinogen abuse

Excludes1: hallucinogen dependence (F16.2–)
hallucinogen use, unspecified (F16.9–)

F16.10 Hallucinogen abuse, uncomplicated

F16.12 Hallucinogen abuse with intoxication

    F16.120 Hallucinogen abuse with intoxication, uncomplicated

    F16.121 Hallucinogen abuse with intoxication with delirium

    F16.122 Hallucinogen abuse with intoxication with perceptual disturbance

    F16.129 Hallucinogen abuse with intoxication, unspecified

F16.14 Hallucinogen abuse with hallucinogen-induced mood disorder

F16.15 Hallucinogen abuse with hallucinogen-induced psychotic disorder

    F16.150 Hallucinogen abuse with hallucinogen-induced psychotic disorder with delusions

    F16.151 Hallucinogen abuse with hallucinogen-induced psychotic disorder with hallucinations

    F16.159 Hallucinogen abuse with hallucinogen-induced psychotic disorder, unspecified

F16.18 Hallucinogen abuse with other hallucinogen-induced disorder

    F16.180 Hallucinogen abuse with hallucinogen-induced anxiety disorder

    F16.183 Hallucinogen abuse with hallucinogen persisting perception disorder (flashbacks)

    F16.188 Hallucinogen abuse with other hallucinogen-induced disorder

F16.19 Hallucinogen abuse with unspecified hallucinogen-induced disorder

F16.2 Hallucinogen dependence

Excludes1: hallucinogen abuse (F16.1–)
hallucinogen use, unspecified (F16.9–)

F16.20 Hallucinogen dependence, uncomplicated

F16.21 Hallucinogen dependence, in remission

F16.22 Hallucinogen dependence with intoxication

F16.220 Hallucinogen dependence with intoxication, uncomplicated

F16.221 Hallucinogen dependence with intoxication with delirium

F16.229 Hallucinogen dependence with intoxication, unspecified

F16.24 Hallucinogen dependence with hallucinogen-induced mood disorder

F16.25 Hallucinogen dependence with hallucinogen-induced psychotic disorder

F16.250 Hallucinogen dependence with hallucinogen-induced psychotic disorder with delusions

F16.251 Hallucinogen dependence with hallucinogen-induced psychotic disorder with hallucinations

F16.259 Hallucinogen dependence with hallucinogen-induced psychotic disorder, unspecified

F16.28 Hallucinogen dependence with other hallucinogen-induced disorder

F16.280 Hallucinogen dependence with hallucinogen-induced anxiety disorder

F16.283 Hallucinogen dependence with hallucinogen persisting perception disorder (flashbacks)

F16.288 Hallucinogen dependence with other hallucinogen-induced disorder

F16.29 Hallucinogen dependence with unspecified hallucinogen-induced disorder

F16.9 Hallucinogen use, unspecified

Excludes1: hallucinogen abuse (F16.1–)
           hallucinogen dependence (F16.2–)

F16.90 Hallucinogen use, unspecified, uncomplicated

F16.92 Hallucinogen use, unspecified with intoxication

F16.920 Hallucinogen use, unspecified with intoxication, uncomplicated

F16.921 Hallucinogen use, unspecified with intoxication with delirium

F16.929 Hallucinogen use, unspecified with intoxication, unspecified

F16.94 Hallucinogen use, unspecified with hallucinogen-induced mood disorder

F16.95 Hallucinogen use, unspecified with hallucinogen-induced psychotic disorder

F16.950 Hallucinogen use, unspecified with hallucinogen-induced psychotic disorder with delusions

F16.951 Hallucinogen use, unspecified with hallucinogen-induced psychotic disorder with hallucinations

F16.959 Hallucinogen use, unspecified with hallucinogen-induced psychotic disorder, unspecified

F16.98 Hallucinogen use, unspecified with other specified hallucinogen-induced disorder

F16.980 Hallucinogen use, unspecified with hallucinogen-induced anxiety disorder

F16.983 Hallucinogen use, unspecified with hallucinogen persisting perception disorder (flashbacks)

F16.988 Hallucinogen use, unspecified with other hallucinogen-induced disorder

F16.99 Hallucinogen use, unspecified with unspecified hallucinogen-induced disorder

F17 Nicotine dependence

Excludes1: history of tobacco dependence (Z87.891) tobacco use NOS (Z72.0)

Excludes2: tobacco use (smoking) during pregnancy, childbirth and the puerperium (O99.33–) toxic effect of nicotine (T65.2–)

F17.2 Nicotine dependence

F17.20 Nicotine dependence, unspecified

F17.200 Nicotine dependence, unspecified, uncomplicated

F17.201 Nicotine dependence, unspecified, in remission

F17.203 Nicotine dependence unspecified, with withdrawal

F17.208 Nicotine dependence, unspecified, with other nicotine-induced disorders

F17.209 Nicotine dependence, unspecified, with unspecified nicotine-induced disorders

F17.21 Nicotine dependence, cigarettes

F17.210 Nicotine dependence, cigarettes, uncomplicated

F17.211 Nicotine dependence, cigarettes, in remission

F17.213 Nicotine dependence, cigarettes, with withdrawal

F17.218 Nicotine dependence, cigarettes, with other nicotine-induced disorders

F17.219 Nicotine dependence, cigarettes, with unspecified nicotine-induced disorders

F17.22 Nicotine dependence, chewing tobacco

F17.220 Nicotine dependence, chewing tobacco, uncomplicated

F17.221 Nicotine dependence, chewing tobacco, in remission

F17.223 Nicotine dependence, chewing tobacco, with withdrawal

F17.228 Nicotine dependence, chewing tobacco, with other nicotine-induced disorders

F17.229 Nicotine dependence, chewing tobacco, with unspecified nicotine-induced disorders

F17.29 Nicotine dependence, other tobacco product

F17.290 Nicotine dependence, other tobacco product, uncomplicated

F17.291 Nicotine dependence, other tobacco product, in remission

F17.293 Nicotine dependence, other tobacco product, with withdrawal

F17.298 Nicotine dependence, other tobacco product, with other nicotine-induced disorders

F17.299 Nicotine dependence, other tobacco product, with unspecified nicotine-induced disorders

F18 Inhalant related disorders

Includes: volatile solvents

F18.1 Inhalant abuse

Excludes1: inhalant dependence (F18.2–)
inhalant use, unspecified (F18.9–)

F18.10 Inhalant abuse, uncomplicated

F18.12 Inhalant abuse with intoxication

F18.120 Inhalant abuse with intoxication, uncomplicated

F18.121 Inhalant abuse with intoxication delirium

F18.129 Inhalant abuse with intoxication, unspecified

F18.14 Inhalant abuse with inhalant-induced mood disorder

F18.15 Inhalant abuse with inhalant-induced psychotic disorder

F18.150 Inhalant abuse with inhalant-induced psychotic disorder with delusions

F18.151 Inhalant abuse with inhalant-induced psychotic disorder with hallucinations

F18.159 Inhalant abuse with inhalant-induced psychotic disorder, unspecified

F18.17 Inhalant abuse with inhalant-induced dementia

F18.18 Inhalant abuse with other inhalant-induced disorders

F18.180 Inhalant abuse with inhalant-induced anxiety disorder

F18.188 Inhalant abuse with other inhalant-induced disorder

F18.19 Inhalant abuse with unspecified inhalant-induced disorder

F18.2 Inhalant dependence

Excludes1: inhalant abuse (F18.1–)
            inhalant use, unspecified (F18.9–)

F18.20 Inhalant dependence, uncomplicated

F18.21 Inhalant dependence, in remission

F18.22 Inhalant dependence with intoxication

   F18.220 Inhalant dependence with intoxication, uncomplicated

   F18.221 Inhalant dependence with intoxication delirium

   F18.229 Inhalant dependence with intoxication, unspecified

F18.24 Inhalant dependence with inhalant-induced mood disorder

F18.25 Inhalant dependence with inhalant-induced psychotic disorder

   F18.250 Inhalant dependence with inhalant-induced psychotic disorder with delusions

   F18.251 Inhalant dependence with inhalant-induced psychotic disorder with hallucinations

   F18.259 Inhalant dependence with inhalant-induced psychotic disorder, unspecified

F18.27 Inhalant dependence with inhalant-induced dementia

F18.28 Inhalant dependence with other inhalant-induced disorders

   F18.280 Inhalant dependence with inhalant-induced anxiety disorder

   F18.288 Inhalant dependence with other inhalant-induced disorder

F18.29 Inhalant dependence with unspecified inhalant-induced disorder

F18.9 Inhalant use, unspecified

Excludes1: inhalant abuse (F18.1–)
inhalant dependence (F18.2–)

F18.90 Inhalant use, unspecified, uncomplicated

F18.92 Inhalant use, unspecified with intoxication

F18.920 Inhalant use, unspecified with intoxication, uncomplicated

F18.921 Inhalant use, unspecified with intoxication with delirium

F18.929 Inhalant use, unspecified with intoxication, unspecified

F18.94 Inhalant use, unspecified with inhalant-induced mood disorder

F18.95 Inhalant use, unspecified with inhalant-induced psychotic disorder

F18.950 Inhalant use, unspecified with inhalant-induced psychotic disorder with delusions

F18.951 Inhalant use, unspecified with inhalant-induced psychotic disorder with hallucinations

F18.959 Inhalant use, unspecified with inhalant-induced psychotic disorder, unspecified

F18.97 Inhalant use, unspecified with inhalant-induced persisting dementia

F18.98 Inhalant use, unspecified with other inhalant-induced disorders

F18.980 Inhalant use, unspecified with inhalant-induced anxiety disorder

F18.988 Inhalant use, unspecified with other inhalant-induced disorder

F18.99 Inhalant use, unspecified with unspecified inhalant-induced disorder

F19 Other psychoactive substance related disorders

    Includes: polysubstance drug use (indiscriminate drug use)

    F19.1 Other psychoactive substance abuse

        Excludes1: other psychoactive substance dependence (F19.2–)
other psychoactive substance use, unspecified (F19.9–)

        F19.10 Other psychoactive substance abuse, uncomplicated

        F19.12 Other psychoactive substance abuse with intoxication

            F19.120 Other psychoactive substance abuse with intoxication, uncomplicated

            F19.121 Other psychoactive substance abuse with intoxication delirium

            F19.122 Other psychoactive substance abuse with intoxication with perceptual disturbances

            F19.129 Other psychoactive substance abuse with intoxication, unspecified

        F19.14 Other psychoactive substance abuse with psychoactive substance-induced mood disorder

        F19.15 Other psychoactive substance abuse with psychoactive substance-induced psychotic disorder

            F19.150 Other psychoactive substance abuse with psychoactive substance-induced psychotic disorder with delusions

            F19.151 Other psychoactive substance abuse with psychoactive substance-induced psychotic disorder with hallucinations

F19.159 Other psychoactive substance abuse with psychoactive substance-induced psychotic disorder, unspecified

F19.16 Other psychoactive substance abuse with psychoactive substance-induced persisting amnestic disorder

F19.17 Other psychoactive substance abuse with psychoactive substance-induced persisting dementia

F19.18 Other psychoactive substance abuse with other psychoactive substance-induced disorders

F19.180 Other psychoactive substance abuse with psychoactive substance-induced anxiety disorder

F19.181 Other psychoactive substance abuse with psychoactive substance-induced sexual dysfunction

F19.182 Other psychoactive substance abuse with psychoactive substance-induced sleep disorder

F19.188 Other psychoactive substance abuse with other psychoactive substance-induced disorder

F19.19 Other psychoactive substance abuse with unspecified psychoactive substance-induced disorder

F19.2 Other psychoactive substance dependence

Excludes1: other psychoactive substance abuse (F19.1–)
other psychoactive substance use, unspecified (F19.9–)

F19.20 Other psychoactive substance dependence, uncomplicated

F19.21 Other psychoactive substance dependence, in remission

F19.22 Other psychoactive substance dependence with intoxication

> Excludes1: other psychoactive substance dependence with withdrawal (F19.23–)

> F19.220 Other psychoactive substance dependence with intoxication, uncomplicated

> F19.221 Other psychoactive substance dependence with intoxication delirium

> F19.222 Other psychoactive substance dependence with intoxication with perceptual disturbance

> F19.229 Other psychoactive substance dependence with intoxication, unspecified

F19.23 Other psychoactive substance dependence with withdrawal

> Excludes1: other psychoactive substance dependence with intoxication (F19.22–)

> F19.230 Other psychoactive substance dependence with withdrawal, uncomplicated

> F19.231 Other psychoactive substance dependence with withdrawal delirium

> F19.232 Other psychoactive substance dependence with withdrawal with perceptual disturbance

> F19.239 Other psychoactive substance dependence with withdrawal, unspecified

F19.24 Other psychoactive substance dependence with psychoactive substance-induced mood disorder

F19.25 Other psychoactive substance dependence with psychoactive substance-induced psychotic disorder

F19.250 Other psychoactive substance dependence with psychoactive substance-induced psychotic disorder with delusions

F19.251 Other psychoactive substance dependence with psychoactive substance-induced psychotic disorder with hallucinations

F19.259 Other psychoactive substance dependence with psychoactive substance-induced psychotic disorder, unspecified

F19.26 Other psychoactive substance dependence with psychoactive substance-induced persisting amnestic disorder

F19.27 Other psychoactive substance dependence with psychoactive substance-induced persisting dementia

F19.28 Other psychoactive substance dependence with other psychoactive substance-induced disorders

F19.280 Other psychoactive substance dependence with psychoactive substance-induced anxiety disorder

F19.281 Other psychoactive substance dependence with psychoactive substance-induced sexual dysfunction

F19.282 Other psychoactive substance dependence with psychoactive substance-induced sleep disorder

F19.288 Other psychoactive substance dependence with other psychoactive substance-induced disorder

F19.29 Other psychoactive substance dependence with unspecified psychoactive substance-induced disorder

F19.9 Other psychoactive substance use, unspecified

Excludes1: other psychoactive substance abuse (F19.1–)
other psychoactive substance dependence (F19.2–)

F19.90 Other psychoactive substance use, unspecified, uncomplicated

F19.92 Other psychoactive substance use, unspecified with intoxication

Excludes1: other psychoactive substance use, unspecified with withdrawal (F19.93)

F19.920 Other psychoactive substance use, unspecified with intoxication, uncomplicated

F19.921 Other psychoactive substance use, unspecified with intoxication with delirium

F19.922 Other psychoactive substance use, unspecified with intoxication with perceptual disturbance

F19.929 Other psychoactive substance use, unspecified with intoxication, unspecified

F19.93 Other psychoactive substance use, unspecified with withdrawal

Excludes1: other psychoactive substance use, unspecified with intoxication (F19.92–)

F19.930 Other psychoactive substance use, unspecified with withdrawal, uncomplicated

F19.931 Other psychoactive substance use, unspecified with withdrawal delirium

F19.932 Other psychoactive substance use, unspecified with withdrawal with perceptual disturbance

F19.939 Other psychoactive substance use, unspecified with withdrawal, unspecified

F19.94 Other psychoactive substance use, unspecified with psychoactive substance-induced mood disorder

F19.95 Other psychoactive substance use, unspecified with psychoactive substance-induced psychotic disorder

F19.950 Other psychoactive substance use, unspecified with psychoactive substance-induced psychotic disorder with delusions

F19.951 Other psychoactive substance use, unspecified with psychoactive substance-induced psychotic disorder with hallucinations

F19.959 Other psychoactive substance use, unspecified with psychoactive substance-induced psychotic disorder, unspecified

F19.96 Other psychoactive substance use, unspecified with psychoactive substance-induced persisting amnestic disorder

F19.97 Other psychoactive substance use, unspecified with psychoactive substance-induced persisting dementia

F19.98 Other psychoactive substance use, unspecified with other psychoactive substance-induced disorders

    F19.980 Other psychoactive substance use, unspecified with psychoactive substance-induced anxiety disorder

    F19.981 Other psychoactive substance use, unspecified with psychoactive substance-induced sexual dysfunction

    F19.982 Other psychoactive substance use, unspecified with psychoactive substance-induced sleep disorder

    F19.988 Other psychoactive substance use, unspecified with other psychoactive substance-induced disorder

F19.99 Other psychoactive substance use, unspecified with unspecified psychoactive substance-induced disorder

Schizophrenia, schizotypal, delusional, and other non-mood psychotic disorders (F20–F29)

F20 Schizophrenia

Excludes1: brief psychotic disorder (F23)
cyclic schizophrenia (F25.0)
mood [affective] disorders with psychotic symptoms (F30.2, F31.2, F31.5, F31.64, F32.3, F33.3)
schizoaffective disorder (F25.–)
schizophrenic reaction NOS (F23)

Excludes2: schizophrenic reaction in:
alcoholism (F10.15–, F10.25–, F10.95–)
brain disease (F06.2)
epilepsy (F06.2)
psychoactive drug use (F11–F19 with .15. .25, .95)
schizotypal disorder (F21)

F20.0 Paranoid schizophrenia

Paraphrenic schizophrenia

Excludes1: involutional paranoid state (F22)
                paranoia (F22)

F20.1 Disorganized schizophrenia

Hebephrenic schizophrenia

Hebephrenia

F20.2 Catatonic schizophrenia

Schizophrenic catalepsy
Schizophrenic catatonia
Schizophrenic flexibilitas cerea

Excludes1: catatonic stupor (R40.1)

F20.3 Undifferentiated schizophrenia

Atypical schizophrenia

Excludes1: acute schizophrenia-like psychotic
                disorder (F23)

Excludes2: post-schizophrenic depression (F32.8)

F20.5 Residual schizophrenia

Restzustand (schizophrenic)
Schizophrenic residual state

F20.8 Other schizophrenia

F20.81 Schizophreniform disorder

Schizophreniform psychosis NOS

F20.89 Other schizophrenia

Cenesthopathic schizophrenia
Simple schizophrenia

F20.9 Schizophrenia, unspecified

F21 Schizotypal disorder

Borderline schizophrenia
Latent schizophrenia
Latent schizophrenic reaction
Prepsychotic schizophrenia
Prodromal schizophrenia
Pseudoneurotic schizophrenia

Pseudopsychopathic schizophrenia
Schizotypal personality disorder

Excludes2: Asperger's syndrome (F84.5)
schizoid personality disorder (F60.1)

F22 Delusional disorders

Delusional dysmorphophobia
Involutional paranoid state
Paranoia
Paranoia querulans
Paranoid psychosis
Paranoid state
Paraphrenia (late)
Sensitiver Beziehungswahn

Excludes1: mood [affective] disorders with psychotic
symptoms (F30.2, F31.2, F31.5, F31.64,
F32.3, F33.3)
paranoid schizophrenia (F20.0)

Excludes2: paranoid personality disorder (F60.0)
paranoid psychosis, psychogenic (F23)
paranoid reaction (F23)

F23 Brief psychotic disorder

Paranoid reaction
Psychogenic paranoid psychosis

Excludes2: mood [affective] disorders with psychotic
symptoms (F30.2, F31.2, F31.5, F31.64,
F32.3, F33.3)

F24 Shared psychotic disorder

Folie à deux
Induced paranoid disorder
Induced psychotic disorder

F25 Schizoaffective disorders

Excludes1: mood [affective] disorders with psychotic symptoms (F30.2, F31.2, F31.5, F31.64, F32.3, F33.3)
schizophrenia (F20.–)

F25.0 Schizoaffective disorder, bipolar type

Cyclic schizophrenia
Schizoaffective disorder, manic type

Schizoaffective disorder, mixed type
Schizoaffective psychosis, bipolar type
Schizophreniform psychosis, manic type

F25.1 Schizoaffective disorder, depressive type

Schizoaffective psychosis, depressive type
Schizophreniform psychosis, depressive type

F25.8 Other schizoaffective disorders

F25.9 Schizoaffective disorder, unspecified

Schizoaffective psychosis NOS

F28 Other psychotic disorder not due to a substance or known physiological condition

Chronic hallucinatory psychosis

F29 Unspecified psychosis not due to a substance or known physiological condition

Psychosis NOS

Excludes1: mental disorder NOS (F99)
unspecified mental disorder due to known
physiological condition (F09)

Mood [affective] disorders (F30–F39)

F30 Manic episode

Includes: bipolar disorder, single manic episode
mixed affective episode

Excludes1: bipolar disorder (F31.–)
major depressive disorder, single episode (F32.–)
major depressive disorder, recurrent (F33.–)

F30.1 Manic episode without psychotic symptoms

F30.10 Manic episode without psychotic symptoms, unspecified

F30.11 Manic episode without psychotic symptoms, mild

F30.12 Manic episode without psychotic symptoms, moderate

F30.13 Manic episode, severe, without psychotic symptoms

F30.2 Manic episode, severe with psychotic symptoms

Manic stupor
Mania with mood-congruent psychotic symptoms
Mania with mood-incongruent psychotic symptoms

F30.3 Manic episode in partial remission

F30.4 Manic episode in full remission

F30.8 Other manic episodes

Hypomania

F30.9 Manic episode, unspecified

Mania NOS

F31 Bipolar disorder

Includes: manic-depressive illness
                    manic-depressive psychosis
                    manic-depressive reaction

Excludes1: bipolar disorder, single manic episode (F30.–)
                      major depressive disorder, single episode (F32.–)
                      major depressive disorder, recurrent (F33.–)

Excludes2: cyclothymia (F34.0)

F31.0 Bipolar disorder, current episode hypomanic

F31.1 Bipolar disorder, current episode manic without psychotic features

F31.10 Bipolar disorder, current episode manic without psychotic features, unspecified

F31.11 Bipolar disorder, current episode manic without psychotic features, mild

F31.12 Bipolar disorder, current episode manic without psychotic features, moderate

F31.13 Bipolar disorder, current episode manic without psychotic features, severe

F31.2 Bipolar disorder, current episode manic severe with psychotic features

Bipolar disorder, current episode manic with mood-congruent psychotic symptoms
Bipolar disorder, current episode manic with mood-incongruent psychotic symptoms

F31.3 Bipolar disorder, current episode depressed, mild or moderate severity

    F31.30 Bipolar disorder, current episode depressed, mild or moderate severity, unspecified

    F31.31 Bipolar disorder, current episode depressed, mild

    F31.32 Bipolar disorder, current episode depressed, moderate

F31.4 Bipolar disorder, current episode depressed, severe, without psychotic features

F31.5 Bipolar disorder, current episode depressed, severe, with psychotic features

Bipolar disorder, current episode depressed with mood-incongruent psychotic symptoms
Bipolar disorder, current episode depressed with mood-congruent psychotic symptoms

F31.6 Bipolar disorder, current episode mixed

    F31.60 Bipolar disorder, current episode mixed, unspecified

    F31.61 Bipolar disorder, current episode mixed, mild

    F31.62 Bipolar disorder, current episode mixed, moderate

    F31.63 Bipolar disorder, current episode mixed, severe, without psychotic features

    F31.64 Bipolar disorder, current episode mixed, severe, with psychotic features

        Bipolar disorder, current episode mixed with mood-congruent psychotic symptoms
        Bipolar disorder, current episode mixed with mood-incongruent psychotic symptoms

F31.7 Bipolar disorder, currently in remission

    F31.70 Bipolar disorder, currently in remission, most recent episode unspecified

    F31.71 Bipolar disorder, in partial remission, most recent episode hypomanic

F31.72 Bipolar disorder, in full remission, most recent episode hypomanic

F31.73 Bipolar disorder, in partial remission, most recent episode manic

F31.74 Bipolar disorder, in full remission, most recent episode manic

F31.75 Bipolar disorder, in partial remission, most recent episode depressed

F31.76 Bipolar disorder, in full remission, most recent episode depressed

F31.77 Bipolar disorder, in partial remission, most recent episode mixed

F31.78 Bipolar disorder, in full remission, most recent episode mixed

F31.8 Other bipolar disorders

F31.81 Bipolar II disorder

F31.89 Other bipolar disorder

Recurrent manic episodes NOS

F31.9 Bipolar disorder, unspecified

F32 Major depressive disorder, single episode

Includes: single episode of agitated depression
single episode of depressive reaction
single episode of major depression
single episode of psychogenic depression
single episode of reactive depression
single episode of vital depression

Excludes1: bipolar disorder (F31.–)
manic episode (F30.–)
recurrent depressive disorder (F33.–)

Excludes2: adjustment disorder (F43.2)

F32.0 Major depressive disorder, single episode, mild

F32.1 Major depressive disorder, single episode, moderate

F32.2 Major depressive disorder, single episode, severe without psychotic features

F32.3 Major depressive disorder, single episode, severe with psychotic features

Single episode of major depression with mood-congruent psychotic symptoms
Single episode of major depression with mood-incongruent psychotic symptoms
Single episode of major depression with psychotic symptoms
Single episode of psychogenic depressive psychosis
Single episode of psychotic depression
Single episode of reactive depressive psychosis

F32.4 Major depressive disorder, single episode, in partial remission

F32.5 Major depressive disorder, single episode, in full remission

F32.8 Other depressive episodes

Atypical depression
Post-schizophrenic depression
Single episode of 'masked' depression NOS

F32.9 Major depressive disorder, single episode, unspecified

Depression NOS
Depressive disorder NOS
Major depression NOS

F33 Major depressive disorder, recurrent

Includes: recurrent episodes of depressive reaction
recurrent episodes of endogenous depression
recurrent episodes of major depression
recurrent episodes of psychogenic depression
recurrent episodes of reactive depression
recurrent episodes of seasonal depressive disorder
recurrent episodes of vital depression

Excludes1: bipolar disorder (F31.–)
manic episode (F30.–)

F33.0 Major depressive disorder, recurrent, mild

F33.1 Major depressive disorder, recurrent, moderate

F33.2 Major depressive disorder, recurrent severe without psychotic features

F33.3 Major depressive disorder, recurrent, severe with psychotic symptoms

Endogenous depression with psychotic symptoms
Recurrent severe episodes of major depression with mood-congruent psychotic symptoms
Recurrent severe episodes of major depression with mood-incongruent psychotic symptoms
Recurrent severe episodes of major depression with psychotic symptoms
Recurrent severe episodes of psychogenic depressive psychosis
Recurrent severe episodes of psychotic depression
Recurrent severe episodes of reactive depressive psychosis

F33.4 Major depressive disorder, recurrent, in remission

F33.40 Major depressive disorder, recurrent, in remission, unspecified

F33.41 Major depressive disorder, recurrent, in partial remission

F33.42 Major depressive disorder, recurrent, in full remission

F33.8 Other recurrent depressive disorders

Recurrent brief depressive episodes

F33.9 Major depressive disorder, recurrent, unspecified

Monopolar depression NOS

F34 Persistent mood [affective] disorders

F34.0 Cyclothymic disorder

Affective personality disorder
Cycloid personality
Cyclothymia
Cyclothymic personality

F34.1 Dysthymic disorder

Depressive neurosis
Depressive personality disorder

Dysthymia
Neurotic depression
Persistent anxiety depression

Excludes2: anxiety depression (mild or not persistent)
(F41.8)

F34.8 Other persistent mood [affective] disorders

F34.9 Persistent mood [affective] disorder, unspecified

F39 Unspecified mood [affective] disorder

Affective psychosis NOS

Anxiety, dissociative, stress-related, somatoform and other nonpsychotic mental disorders (F40–F48)

F40 Phobic anxiety disorders

F40.0 Agoraphobia

F40.00 Agoraphobia, unspecified

F40.01 Agoraphobia with panic disorder

Panic disorder with agoraphobia

Excludes1: panic disorder without
agoraphobia (F41.0)

F40.02 Agoraphobia without panic disorder

F40.1 Social phobias

Anthropophobia
Social anxiety disorder of childhood
Social neurosis

F40.10 Social phobia, unspecified

F40.11 Social phobia, generalized

F40.2 Specific (isolated) phobias

Excludes2: dysmorphophobia (nondelusional)
(F45.22)
nosophobia (F45.22)

F40.21 Animal type phobia

F40.210 Arachnophobia

Fear of spiders

F40.218 Other animal type phobia

F40.22 **Natural environment type phobia**

    F40.220 **Fear of thunderstorms**

    F40.228 **Other natural environment type phobia**

F40.23 **Blood, injection, injury type phobia**

    F40.230 **Fear of blood**

    F40.231 **Fear of injections and transfusions**

    F40.232 **Fear of other medical care**

    F40.233 **Fear of injury**

F40.24 **Situational type phobia**

    F40.240 **Claustrophobia**

    F40.241 **Acrophobia**

    F40.242 **Fear of bridges**

    F40.243 **Fear of flying**

    F40.248 **Other situational type phobia**

F40.29 **Other specified phobia**

    F40.290 **Androphobia**

        Fear of men

    F40.291 **Gynephobia**

        Fear of women

    F40.298 **Other specified phobia**

F40.8 **Other phobic anxiety disorders**

Phobic anxiety disorder of childhood

F40.9 **Phobic anxiety disorder, unspecified**

Phobia NOS
Phobic state NOS

F41 **Other anxiety disorders**

Excludes2: anxiety in:
    acute stress reaction (F43.0)
    transient adjustment reaction (F43.2)
    neurasthenia (F48.8)
    psychophysiologic disorders (F45.–)
    separation anxiety (F93.0)

F41.0 Panic disorder [episodic paroxysmal anxiety] without agoraphobia

Panic attack
Panic state

Excludes1: panic disorder with agoraphobia (F40.01)

F41.1 Generalized anxiety disorder

Anxiety neurosis
Anxiety reaction
Anxiety state
Overanxious disorder

Excludes2: neurasthenia (F48.8)

F41.3 Other mixed anxiety disorders

F41.8 Other specified anxiety disorders

Anxiety depression (mild or not persistent)
Anxiety hysteria
Mixed anxiety and depressive disorder

F41.9 Anxiety disorder, unspecified

Anxiety NOS

F42 Obsessive-compulsive disorder

Anancastic neurosis
Obsessive-compulsive neurosis

Excludes2: obsessive-compulsive personality (disorder) (F60.5)
obsessive-compulsive symptoms occurring in depression (F32–F33)
obsessive-compulsive symptoms occurring in schizophrenia (F20.–)

F43 Reaction to severe stress, and adjustment disorders

F43.0 Acute stress reaction

Acute crisis reaction
Acute reaction to stress
Combat and operational stress reaction
Combat fatigue
Crisis state
Psychic shock

F43.1 Post-traumatic stress disorder (PTSD)

Traumatic neurosis

F43.10 Post-traumatic stress disorder, unspecified

F43.11 Post-traumatic stress disorder, acute

F43.12 Post-traumatic stress disorder, chronic

F43.2 **Adjustment disorders**

Culture shock
Grief reaction
Hospitalism in children

Excludes2: separation anxiety disorder of childhood (F93.0)

F43.20 Adjustment disorder, unspecified

F43.21 Adjustment disorder with depressed mood

F43.22 Adjustment disorder with anxiety

F43.23 Adjustment disorder with mixed anxiety and depressed mood

F43.24 Adjustment disorder with disturbance of conduct

F43.25 Adjustment disorder with mixed disturbance of emotions and conduct

F43.29 Adjustment disorder with other symptoms

F43.8 **Other reactions to severe stress**

F43.9 **Reaction to severe stress, unspecified**

F44 **Dissociative and conversion disorders**

Includes: conversion hysteria
conversion reaction
hysteria
hysterical psychosis

Excludes2: malingering [conscious simulation] (Z76.5)

F44.0 **Dissociative amnesia**

Excludes1: amnesia NOS (R41.3)
anterograde amnesia (R41.1)
retrograde amnesia (R41.2)

Excludes2: alcohol-or other psychoactive substance-induced amnestic disorder (F10, F13, F19 with .26, .96)
amnestic disorder due to known physiological condition (F04)
postictal amnesia in epilepsy (G40.–)

F44.1 Dissociative fugue

Excludes2: postictal fugue in epilepsy (G40.–)

F44.2 Dissociative stupor

Excludes1: catatonic stupor (R40.1)
stupor NOS (R40.1)

Excludes2: catatonic disorder due to known physiological condition (F06.1)
depressive stupor (F32, F33)
manic stupor (F30, F31)

F44.4 Conversion disorder with motor symptom or deficit

Dissociative motor disorders
Psychogenic aphonia
Psychogenic dysphonia

F44.5 Conversion disorder with seizures or convulsions

Dissociative convulsions

F44.6 Conversion disorder with sensory symptom or deficit

Dissociative anesthesia and sensory loss
Psychogenic deafness

F44.7 Conversion disorder with mixed symptom presentation

F44.8 Other dissociative and conversion disorders

F44.81 Dissociative identity disorder

Multiple personality disorder

F44.89 Other dissociative and conversion disorders

Ganser's syndrome
Psychogenic confusion
Psychogenic twilight state
Trance and possession disorders

F44.9 Dissociative and conversion disorder, unspecified

Dissociative disorder NOS

F45 Somatoform disorders

Excludes2: dissociative and conversion disorders (F44.–)

factitious disorders (F68.1–)

hair-plucking (F63.3)

lalling (F80.0)

lisping (F80.0)

malingering [conscious simulation] (Z76.5)

nail-biting (F98.8)

psychological or behavioral factors associated with disorders or diseases classified elsewhere (F54)

sexual dysfunction, not due to a substance or known physiological condition (F52.–)

thumb-sucking (F98.8)

tic disorders (in childhood and adolescence) (F95.–)

Tourette's syndrome (F95.2)

trichotillomania (F63.3)

F45.0 Somatization disorder

Briquet's disorder

Multiple psychosomatic disorder

F45.1 Undifferentiated somatoform disorder

Undifferentiated psychosomatic disorder

F45.2 Hypochondriacal disorders

Excludes2: delusional dysmorphophobia (F22)

fixed delusions about bodily functions or shape (F22)

F45.20 Hypochondriacal disorder, unspecified

F45.21 Hypochondriasis

Hypochondriacal neurosis

F45.22 Body dysmorphic disorder

Dysmorphophobia (nondelusional)

Nosophobia

F45.29 Other hypochondriacal disorders

F45.4 Pain disorders related to psychological factors

Excludes1: pain NOS (R52)

F45.41 Pain disorder exclusively related to psychological factors

Somatoform pain disorder (persistent)

F45.42 Pain disorder with related psychological factors

Code also associated acute or chronic pain (G89.–)

F45.8 Other somatoform disorders

Psychogenic dysmenorrhea
Psychogenic dysphagia, including 'globus hystericus'
Psychogenic pruritus
Psychogenic torticollis
Somatoform autonomic dysfunction
Teeth grinding

Excludes1: sleep related teeth grinding (G47.63)

F45.9 Somatoform disorder, unspecified

Psychosomatic disorder NOS

F48 Other nonpsychotic mental disorders

F48.1 Depersonalization-derealization syndrome

F48.2 Pseudobulbar affect

Involuntary emotional expression disorder

Code first underlying cause, if known, such as:
amyotrophic lateral sclerosis (G12.21)
multiple sclerosis (G35)
sequelae of cerebrovascular disease (I69.–)
sequelae of traumatic intracranial injury (S06.–)

F48.8 Other specified nonpsychotic mental disorders

Dhat syndrome
Neurasthenia
Occupational neurosis, including writer's cramp
Psychasthenia
Psychasthenic neurosis
Psychogenic syncope

F48.9 Nonpsychotic mental disorder, unspecified

Neurosis NOS

Behavioral syndromes associated with physiological disturbances and physical factors (F50–F59)

F50 Eating disorders

Excludes1: anorexia NOS (R63.0)
feeding difficulties (R63.3)
polyphagia (R63.2)

Excludes2: feeding disorder in infancy or childhood (F98.2-)

F50.0 Anorexia nervosa

Excludes1: loss of appetite (R63.0)
psychogenic loss of appetite (F50.8)

F50.00 Anorexia nervosa, unspecified

F50.01 Anorexia nervosa, restricting type

F50.02 Anorexia nervosa, binge eating/purging type

Excludes1: bulimia nervosa (F50.2)

F50.2 Bulimia nervosa

Bulimia NOS
Hyperorexia nervosa

Excludes1: anorexia nervosa, binge eating/purging type (F50.02)

F50.8 Other eating disorders

Pica in adults
Psychogenic loss of appetite
Excludes2: pica of infancy and childhood (F98.3)

F50.9 Eating disorder, unspecified

Atypical anorexia nervosa
Atypical bulimia nervosa

F51 Sleep disorders not due to a substance or known physiological condition

Excludes2: organic sleep disorders (G47.–)

F51.0 Insomnia not due to a substance or known physiological condition

Excludes2: alcohol related insomnia (F10.182, F10.282, F10.982)

drug-related insomnia (F11.182, F11.282, F11.982, F13.182, F13.282, F13.982, F14.182, F14.282, F14.982, F15.182, F15.282, F15.982, F19.182, F19.282, F19.982)
insomnia NOS (G47.0–)
insomnia due to known physiological condition (G47.0–)
organic insomnia (G47.0–)
sleep deprivation (Z72.820)

F51.01 Primary insomnia

Idiopathic insomnia

F51.02 Adjustment insomnia

F51.03 Paradoxical insomnia

F51.04 Psychophysiologic insomnia

F51.05 Insomnia due to other mental disorder

Code also associated mental disorder

F51.09 Other insomnia not due to a substance or known physiological condition

F51.1 Hypersomnia not due to a substance or known physiological condition

Excludes2: alcohol related hypersomnia (F10.182, F10.282, F10.982)
drug-related hypersomnia (F11.182, F11.282, F11.982, F13.182, F13.282, F13.982, F14.182, F14.282, F14.982, F15.182, F15.282, F15.982, F19.182, F19.282, F19.982)
hypersomnia NOS (G47.10)
hypersomnia due to known physiological condition (G47.10)
idiopathic hypersomnia (G47.11, G47.12)
narcolepsy (G47.4–)

F51.11 **Primary hypersomnia**

F51.12 **Insufficient sleep syndrome**

Excludes1: sleep deprivation (Z72.820)

F51.13 **Hypersomnia due to other mental disorder**

Code also associated mental disorder

F51.19 **Other hypersomnia not due to a substance or known physiological condition**

F51.3 **Sleepwalking [somnambulism]**

F51.4 **Sleep terrors [night terrors]**

F51.5 **Nightmare disorder**

Dream anxiety disorder

F51.8 **Other sleep disorders not due to a substance or known physiological condition**

F51.9 **Sleep disorder not due to a substance or known physiological condition, unspecified**

Emotional sleep disorder NOS

F52 **Sexual dysfunction not due to a substance or known physiological condition**

Excludes2: Dhat syndrome (F48.8)

F52.0 **Hypoactive sexual desire disorder**

Anhedonia (sexual)
Lack or loss of sexual desire
Excludes1: decreased libido (R68.82)

F52.1 **Sexual aversion disorder**

Sexual aversion and lack of sexual enjoyment

F52.2 **Sexual arousal disorders**

Failure of genital response

F52.21 **Male erectile disorder**
Psychogenic impotence

Excludes1: impotence of organic origin (N52.–)
impotence NOS (N52.–)

F52.22 **Female sexual arousal disorder**

Frigidity

F52.3 Orgasmic disorder

Inhibited orgasm
Psychogenic anorgasmy

F52.31 Female orgasmic disorder

F52.32 Male orgasmic disorder

F52.4 Premature ejaculation

F52.5 Vaginismus not due to a substance or known physiological condition

Psychogenic vaginismus

Excludes2: vaginismus (due to a known physiological condition) (N94.2)

F52.6 Dyspareunia not due to a substance or known physiological condition

Psychogenic dyspareunia

Excludes2: dyspareunia (due to a known physiological condition) (N94.1)

F52.8 Other sexual dysfunction not due to a substance or known physiological condition

Excessive sexual drive
Nymphomania
Satyriasis

F52.9 Unspecified sexual dysfunction not due to a substance or known physiological condition

Sexual dysfunction NOS

F53 Puerperal psychosis

Postpartum depression

Excludes1: mood disorders with psychotic features (F30.2, F31.2, F31.5, F31.64, F32.3, F33.3)
postpartum dysphoria (O90.6)
psychosis in schizophrenia, schizotypal, delusional, and other psychotic disorders (F20–F29)

F54 Psychological and behavioral factors associated with disorders or diseases classified elsewhere

Psychological factors affecting physical conditions

Code first the associated physical disorder, such as:
asthma (J45.–)
dermatitis (L23–L25)
gastric ulcer (K25.–)
mucous colitis (K58.–)
ulcerative colitis (K51.–)
urticaria (L50.–)

Excludes2: tension-type headache (G44.2)

F55 Abuse of non-psychoactive substances

Excludes2: abuse of psychoactive substances (F10–F19)

F55.0 Abuse of antacids

F55.1 Abuse of herbal or folk remedies

F55.2 Abuse of laxatives

F55.3 Abuse of steroids or hormones

F55.4 Abuse of vitamins

F55.8 Abuse of other non-psychoactive substances

F59 Unspecified behavioral syndromes associated with physiological disturbances and physical factors

Psychogenic physiological dysfunction NOS

Disorders of adult personality and behavior (F60–F69)

F60 Specific personality disorders

F60.0 Paranoid personality disorder
Expansive paranoid personality (disorder)
Fanatic personality (disorder)
Querulant personality (disorder)
Paranoid personality (disorder)
Sensitive paranoid personality (disorder)
Excludes2: paranoia (F22)
paranoia querulans (F22)
paranoid psychosis (F22)
paranoid schizophrenia (F20.0)
paranoid state (F22)

F60.1 Schizoid personality disorder

Excludes2: Asperger's syndrome (F84.5)
delusional disorder (F22)
schizoid disorder of childhood (F84.5)

schizophrenia (F20.–)
schizotypal disorder (F21)

F60.2 Antisocial personality disorder
Amoral personality (disorder)
Asocial personality (disorder)
Dissocial personality disorder
Psychopathic personality (disorder)
Sociopathic personality (disorder)

Excludes1: conduct disorders (F91.–)

Excludes2: borderline personality disorder (F60.3)

F60.3 Borderline personality disorder
Aggressive personality (disorder)
Emotionally unstable personality disorder
Explosive personality (disorder)

Excludes2: antisocial personality disorder (F60.2)

F60.4 Histrionic personality disorder

Hysterical personality (disorder)
Psychoinfantile personality (disorder)

F60.5 Obsessive-compulsive personality disorder
Anankastic personality (disorder)
Compulsive personality (disorder)
Obsessional personality (disorder)

Excludes2: obsessive-compulsive disorder (F42)

F60.6 Avoidant personality disorder

Anxious personality disorder

F60.7 Dependent personality disorder
Asthenic personality (disorder)
Inadequate personality (disorder)
Passive personality (disorder)

F60.8 Other specific personality disorders

F60.81 Narcissistic personality disorder

F60.89 Other specific personality disorders
Eccentric personality disorder
'Haltlose' type personality disorder
Immature personality disorder
Passive-aggressive personality disorder
Psychoneurotic personality disorder
Self-defeating personality disorder

F60.9 Personality disorder, unspecified

Character disorder NOS
Character neurosis NOS
Pathological personality NOS

F63 Impulse disorders

Excludes2: habitual excessive use of alcohol or psycho-active substances (F10–F19)
impulse disorders involving sexual behavior (F65.–)

F63.0 Pathological gambling

Compulsive gambling

Excludes1: gambling and betting NOS (Z72.6)

Excludes2: excessive gambling by manic patients (F30, F31)
gambling in antisocial personality disorder (F60.2)

F63.1 Pyromania

Pathological fire-setting

Excludes2: fire-setting (by) (in):
adult with antisocial personality disorder (F60.2)
alcohol or psychoactive substance intoxication (F10–F19)
conduct disorders (F91.–)
mental disorders due to known physiological condition (F01–F09)
schizophrenia (F20.–)

F63.2 Kleptomania

Pathological stealing

Excludes1: shoplifting as the reason for observation for suspected mental disorder (Z03.8)

Excludes2: depressive disorder with stealing (F31–F33)
stealing due to underlying mental condition-code to mental condition
stealing in mental disorders due to known physiological condition (F01–F09)

F63.3 Trichotillomania

Hair plucking

Excludes2: other stereotyped movement disorder (F98.4)

F63.8 Other impulse disorders

F63.81 Intermittent explosive disorder

F63.89 Other impulse disorders

F63.9 Impulse disorder, unspecified

Impulse control disorder NOS

F64 Gender identity disorders

F64.1 Gender identity disorder in adolescence and adulthood

Dual role transvestism
Transsexualism

Use additional code to identify sex reassignment status (Z87.890)

Excludes1: gender identity disorder in childhood (F64.2)

Excludes2: fetishistic transvestism (F65.1)

F64.2 Gender identity disorder of childhood

Excludes1: gender identity disorder in adolescence and adulthood (F64.1)

Excludes2: sexual maturation disorder (F66)

F64.8 Other gender identity disorders

F64.9 Gender identity disorder, unspecified

Gender-role disorder NOS

F65 Paraphilias

F65.0 Fetishism

F65.1 Transvestic fetishism

Fetishistic transvestism

F65.2 Exhibitionism

F65.3 Voyeurism

F65.4 Pedophilia

F65.5 Sadomasochism

    F65.50 Sadomasochism, unspecified

    F65.51 Sexual masochism

    F65.52 Sexual sadism

F65.8 Other paraphilias

    F65.81 Frotteurism

    F65.89 Other paraphilias

        Necrophilia

F65.9 Paraphilia, unspecified

    Sexual deviation NOS

F66 Other sexual disorders

Sexual maturation disorder

Sexual relationship disorder

F68 Other disorders of adult personality and behavior

F68.1 Factitious disorder

Compensation neurosis
Elaboration of physical symptoms for psychological
reasons
Hospital hopper syndrome
Münchausen's syndrome
Peregrinating patient

Excludes2: factitial dermatitis (L98.1)
               person feigning illness (with obvious
               motivation) (Z76.5)

    F68.10 Factitious disorder, unspecified

    F68.11 Factitious disorder with predominantly
           psychological signs and symptoms

    F68.12 Factitious disorder with predominantly
           physical signs and symptoms

    F68.13 Factitious disorder with combined psycho-
           logical and physical signs and symptoms

F68.8 Other specified disorders of adult personality and
behavior

F69 Unspecified disorder of adult personality and behavior

Intellectual Disabilities (F70–F79)

Code first any associated physical or developmental disorders

Excludes1: borderline intellectual functioning, IQ above 70 to 84 (R41.83)

F70 Mild intellectual disabilities

IQ level 50–55 to approximately 70
Mild mental subnormality

F71 Moderate intellectual disabilities

IQ level 35–40 to 50–55
Moderate mental subnormality

F72 Severe intellectual disabilities

IQ 20–25 to 35–40
Severe mental subnormality

F73 Profound intellectual disabilities

IQ level below 20–25
Profound mental subnormality

F78 Other intellectual disabilities

F79 Unspecified intellectual disabilities

Mental deficiency NOS
Mental subnormality NOS

Pervasive and specific developmental disorders (F80–F89)

F80 Specific developmental disorders of speech and language

F80.0 Phonological disorder

Dyslalia
Functional speech articulation disorder
Lalling
Lisping
Phonological developmental disorder
Speech articulation developmental disorder

Excludes1: speech articulation impairment due to aphasia NOS (R47.01)
speech articulation impairment due to apraxia (R48.2)

Excludes2: speech articulation impairment due to hearing loss (F80.4)

speech articulation impairment due to intellectual disabilities (F70–F79)

speech articulation impairment with expressive language developmental disorder (F80.1)

speech articulation impairment with mixed receptive expressive language developmental disorder (F80.2)

F80.1 Expressive language disorder

Developmental dysphasia or aphasia, expressive type

Excludes1: mixed receptive-expressive language disorder (F80.2)

dysphasia and aphasia NOS (R47.–)

Excludes2: acquired aphasia with epilepsy [Landau-Kleffner] (G40.80–)

selective mutism (F94.0)

intellectual disabilities (F70–F79)

pervasive developmental disorders (F84.–)

F80.2 Mixed receptive-expressive language disorder

Developmental dysphasia or aphasia, receptive type

Developmental Wernicke's aphasia

Excludes1: central auditory processing disorder (H93.25)

dysphasia or aphasia NOS (R47.–)

expressive language disorder (F80.1)

expressive type dysphasia or aphasia (F80.1)

word deafness (H93.25)

Excludes2: acquired aphasia with epilepsy [Landau-Kleffner] (G40.80–)

pervasive developmental disorders (F84.–)

selective mutism (F94.0)

intellectual disabilities (F70–F79)

F80.4   Speech and language development delay due to hearing loss

Code also type of hearing loss (H90.–, H91.–)

F80.8   Other developmental disorders of speech and language

F80.81   Childhood onset fluency disorder

Cluttering NOS
Stuttering NOS

Excludes1: adult onset fluency disorder (F98.5)
fluency disorder in conditions classified elsewhere (R47.82)
fluency disorder (stuttering) following cerebrovascular disease (I69. with final characters –23)

F80.89   Other developmental disorders of speech and language

F80.9   Developmental disorder of speech and language, unspecified

Communication disorder NOS
Language disorder NOS

F81   Specific developmental disorders of scholastic skills

F81.0   Specific reading disorder

'Backward reading'
Developmental dyslexia
Specific reading retardation

Excludes1: alexia NOS (R48.0)
dyslexia NOS (R48.0)

F81.2   Mathematics disorder

Developmental acalculia
Developmental arithmetical disorder
Developmental Gerstmann's syndrome

Excludes1: acalculia NOS (R48.8)

Excludes2: arithmetical difficulties associated with a reading disorder (F81.0)

arithmetical difficulties associated with a spelling disorder (F81.81)
arithmetical difficulties due to inadequate teaching (Z55.8)

F81.8 Other developmental disorders of scholastic skills

F81.81 Disorder of written expression

Specific spelling disorder

F81.89 Other developmental disorders of scholastic skills

F81.9 Developmental disorder of scholastic skills, unspecified

Knowledge acquisition disability NOS
Learning disability NOS
Learning disorder NOS

F82 Specific developmental disorder of motor function

Clumsy child syndrome
Developmental coordination disorder
Developmental dyspraxia

Excludes1: abnormalities of gait and mobility (R26.–)
lack of coordination (R27.–)

Excludes2: lack of coordination secondary to intellectual disabilities (F70–F79)

F84 Pervasive developmental disorders

Use additional code to identify any associated medical condition and intellectual disabilities.

F84.0 Autistic disorder

Infantile autism
Infantile psychosis
Kanner's syndrome

Excludes1: Asperger's syndrome (F84.5)

F84.2 Rett's syndrome

Excludes1: Asperger's syndrome (F84.5)
Autistic disorder (F84.0)
Other childhood disintegrative disorder (F84.3)

F84.3 Other childhood disintegrative disorder

Dementia infantilis
Disintegrative psychosis
Heller's syndrome
Symbiotic psychosis

Use additional code to identify any associated neurological condition.

Excludes1: Asperger's syndrome (F84.5)
Autistic disorder (F84.0)
Rett's syndrome (F84.2)

F84.5 Asperger's syndrome

Asperger's disorder
Autistic psychopathy
Schizoid disorder of childhood

F84.8 Other pervasive developmental disorders

Overactive disorder associated with intellectual disabilities and stereotyped movements

F84.9 Pervasive developmental disorder, unspecified

Atypical autism

F88 Other disorders of psychological development

Developmental agnosia

F89 Unspecified disorder of psychological development

Developmental disorder NOS

Behavioral and emotional disorders with onset usually occurring in childhood and adolescence (F90–F98)

Note: Codes within categories F90–F98 may be used regardless of the age of a patient. These disorders generally have onset within the childhood or adolescent years, but may continue throughout life or not be diagnosed until adulthood

F90 Attention-deficit hyperactivity disorders

Includes: attention deficit disorder with hyperactivity
attention deficit syndrome with hyperactivity

Excludes2: anxiety disorders (F40.–, F41.–)
mood [affective] disorders (F30–F39)
pervasive developmental disorders (F84.–)
schizophrenia (F20.–)

F90.0 Attention-deficit hyperactivity disorder, predominantly inattentive type

F90.1 Attention-deficit hyperactivity disorder, predominantly hyperactive type

F90.2 Attention-deficit hyperactivity disorder, combined type

F90.8 Attention-deficit hyperactivity disorder, other type

F90.9 Attention-deficit hyperactivity disorder, unspecified type

Attention-deficit hyperactivity disorder of childhood or adolescence NOS

Attention-deficit hyperactivity disorder NOS

F91 Conduct disorders

Excludes1: antisocial behavior (Z72.81–)
antisocial personality disorder (F60.2)

Excludes2: conduct problems associated with attention-deficit hyperactivity disorder (F90.–)
mood [affective] disorders (F30–F39)
pervasive developmental disorders (F84.–)
schizophrenia (F20.–)

F91.0 Conduct disorder confined to family context

F91.1 Conduct disorder, childhood-onset type

Unsocialized conduct disorder
Conduct disorder, solitary aggressive type
Unsocialized aggressive disorder

F91.2 Conduct disorder, adolescent-onset type

Socialized conduct disorder
Conduct disorder, group type

F91.3 Oppositional defiant disorder

F91.8 Other conduct disorders

F91.9 Conduct disorder, unspecified

Behavioral disorder NOS
Conduct disorder NOS
Disruptive behavior disorder NOS

F93 Emotional disorders with onset specific to childhood

F93.0 Separation anxiety disorder of childhood

Excludes2: mood [affective] disorders (F30–F39)
nonpsychotic mental disorders (F40–F48)
phobic anxiety disorder of childhood (F40.8)
social phobia (F40.1)

F93.8 Other childhood emotional disorders

Identity disorder

Excludes2: gender identity disorder of childhood (F64.2)

F93.9 Childhood emotional disorder, unspecified

F94 Disorders of social functioning with onset specific to childhood and adolescence

F94.0 Selective mutism

Elective mutism

Excludes2: pervasive developmental disorders (F84.–)
schizophrenia (F20.–)
specific developmental disorders of speech and language (F80.–)
transient mutism as part of separation anxiety in young children (F93.0)

F94.1 Reactive attachment disorder of childhood

Use additional code to identify any associated failure to thrive or growth retardation

Excludes1: disinhibited attachment disorder of childhood (F94.2)
normal variation in pattern of selective attachment

Excludes2: Asperger's syndrome (F84.5)
maltreatment syndromes (T74.–)
sexual or physical abuse in childhood, resulting in psychosocial problems (Z62.81–)

F94.2 Disinhibited attachment disorder of childhood

Affectionless psychopathy
Institutional syndrome

Excludes1: reactive attachment disorder of childhood (F94.1)

Excludes2: Asperger's syndrome (F84.5)
attention-deficit hyperactivity disorders (F90.–)
hospitalism in children (F43.2–)

F94.8 Other childhood disorders of social functioning

F94.9 Childhood disorder of social functioning, unspecified

F95 Tic disorder

F95.0 Transient tic disorder

F95.1 Chronic motor or vocal tic disorder

F95.2 Tourette's disorder

Combined vocal and multiple motor tic disorder [de la Tourette]
Tourette's syndrome

F95.8 Other tic disorders

F95.9 Tic disorder, unspecified

Tic NOS

F98 Other behavioral and emotional disorders with onset usually occurring in childhood and adolescence

Excludes2: breath-holding spells (R06.89)
gender identity disorder of childhood (F64.2)
Kleine-Levin syndrome (G47.13)
obsessive-compulsive disorder (F42)
sleep disorders not due to a substance or known physiological condition (F51.–)

F98.0 Enuresis not due to a substance or known physio-logical condition

Enuresis (primary) (secondary) of nonorganic origin
Functional enuresis
Psychogenic enuresis
Urinary incontinence of nonorganic origin

Excludes1: enuresis NOS (R32)

F98.1 Encopresis not due to a substance or known physiological condition

Functional encopresis
Incontinence of feces of nonorganic origin
Psychogenic encopresis

Use additional code to identify the cause of any coexisting constipation.

Excludes1: encopresis NOS (R15.–)

F98.2 Other feeding disorders of infancy and childhood

Excludes1: feeding difficulties (R63.3)

Excludes2: anorexia nervosa and other eating disorders (F50.–)
feeding problems of newborn (P92.–)
pica of infancy or childhood (F98.3)

F98.21 Rumination disorder of infancy

F98.29 Other feeding disorders of infancy and early childhood

F98.3 Pica of infancy and childhood

F98.4 Stereotyped movement disorders

Stereotype/habit disorder

Excludes1: abnormal involuntary movements (R25.–)

Excludes2: compulsions in obsessive-compulsive disorder (F42)
hair plucking (F63.3)
movement disorders of organic origin (G20–G25)
nail-biting (F98.8)
nose-picking (F98.8)
stereotypies that are part of a broader psychiatric condition (F01–F95)
thumb-sucking (F98.8)
tic disorders (F95.–)
trichotillomania (F63.3)

F98.5 Adult onset fluency disorder

Excludes1: childhood onset fluency disorder (F80.81)
dysphasia (R47.02)

fluency disorder in conditions classified elsewhere (R47.82)
fluency disorder (stuttering) following cerebrovascular disease (I69. with final characters –23)
tic disorders (F95.–)

F98.8 Other specified behavioral and emotional disorders with onset usually occurring in childhood and adolescence

Excessive masturbation
Nail-biting
Nose-picking
Thumb-sucking

F98.9 Unspecified behavioral and emotional disorders with onset usually occurring in childhood and adolescence

Unspecified mental disorder (F99)

F99 Mental disorder, not otherwise specified

Mental illness NOS

Excludes1: unspecified mental disorder due to known physiological condition (F09)

Glossary of Abbreviations

AMA	American Medical Association
APA	American Psychological Association
CDC	Centers for Disease Control and Prevention
CDDG	Clinical Descriptions and Diagnostic Guidelines
CHPS	Center for Health Policy Studies
CMS	Centers for Medicare and Medicaid Services
DSM	Diagnostic and Statistical Manual of Mental Disorders
GEMs	General Equivalence Mappings
HHS	Department of Health and Human Services
HIPAA	Health Insurance Portability and Accountability Act
ICD	International Classification of Diseases
ISI	International Statistical Institute
IUPsyS	International Union of Psychological Science
NCHS	National Center for Health Statistics
NCVHS	National Committee on Vital and Health Statistics
NICE	National Institute for Health and Care Excellence
NIH	National Institutes of Health
WHA	World Health Assembly
WHO	World Health Organization
WPA	World Psychiatric Association

References

ADMINDXRW. (2013, June 12). Comparison between classifications and codings in ICD–10–CM and ICD–10 [Online forum comment]. Retrieved from http://wp.me/pKrrB-3iT

American Psychiatric Association. (1968). *Diagnostic and statistical manual of mental disorders* (2nd ed.). Washington, DC: Author.

American Psychiatric Association. (1980). *Diagnostic and statistical manual of mental disorders* (3rd ed.). Washington, DC: Author.

American Psychiatric Association. (1994). *Diagnostic and statistical manual of mental disorders* (4th ed.). Washington, DC: Author.

American Psychiatric Association. (2000). *Diagnostic and statistical manual of mental disorders* (4th ed., text rev.). Washington, DC: Author.

American Psychiatric Association. (2013a). *Diagnostic and statistical manual of mental disorders* (5th ed.). Arlington, VA: Author.

American Psychiatric Association. (2013b). *Frequently asked questions*. Retrieved from http://www.dsm5.org/Documents/FAQ%20for%20Clinicians%208-1-13.pdf

American Psychiatric Association. (2013c). *Personality disorders*. Retrieved from http://www.dsm5.org/Documents/Personality%20Disorders%20Fact%20Sheet.pdf

American Psychological Association. (Producer). (2013). *Understanding DSM–5 and the ICD: What psychologists need to know.* Available

from http://apa.bizvision.com/product//understandingthe
dsm5andtheicdwhatpsychologistsneedtoknow(8479)

Andrews, G., Goldberg, D. P., Krueger, R. F., Carpenter, W. T., Jr.,
Hyman, S. E., Sachdev, P., & Pine, D. S. (2009). Exploring the
feasibility of a meta-structure for DSM–V and ICD–11: Could
it improve utility and validity? *Psychological Medicine, 39,*
1993–2000. doi:10.1017/S0033291709990250

APA Presidential Task Force on Evidence-Based Practice. (2006).
Evidence-based practice in psychology. *American Psychologist,
61,* 271–285. doi:10.1037/0003-066X.61.4.271

Bullock, M. (2012). Reaching out internationally—Where are we
now? *Psychology International.* Retrieved from http://www.apa.
org/international/pi/2012/10/column.aspx

Centers for Disease Control and Prevention. (2011). *ICD–9–CM.*
Retrieved from http://www.cdc.gov/nchs/icd/icd9cm.htm

Centers for Disease Control and Prevention. (2013). *ICD–10–CM
official guidelines for coding and reporting.* Retrieved from http://
www.cdc.gov/nchs/data/icd9/icd10cm_guidelines_2014.pdf

Centers for Disease Control and Prevention. (2014). *ICD–10–CM.*
Retrieved from http://www.cdc.gov/nchs/icd/icd10cm.htm
#icd2014

Centers for Medicare and Medicaid Services. (1998). *The ICD–10–
CM Procedure Coding System.* Retrieved from http://www.cms.
gov/Medicare/Coding/ICD10/2013-ICD-10-PCS-GEMs.html

Centers for Medicare and Medicaid Services. (2012a). *FAQs: Versions
5010 and D.0 upgrade basics.* http://www.cms.gov/Medicare/
Coding/ICD10/downloads/Versions5010D0FAQs.pdf

Centers for Medicare and Medicaid Services. (2012b). *The ICD planning checklist.* Retrieved from http://www.cms.gov/Medicare/
Coding/ICD10/Downloads/ICD10PlanningChecklist.pdf

Centers for Medicare and Medicaid Services. (2012c). *New health
care standards to save up to $6 billion.* Retrieved from http://www.
cms.gov/apps/media/press/release.asp?Counter=4444&intNum
PerPage=10&checkDate=&checkKey=&srchType=1&numDays=
3500&srchOpt=0&srchData=&keywordType=All&chkNews

Type=1%2C+2%2C+3%2C+4%2C+5&intPage=&showAll=
&pYear=&year=&desc=&cboOrder=date

Centers for Medicare and Medicaid Services. (2013). *Frequently asked questions* (FAQ 1817). Retrieved from https://questions.cms.gov/faq.php?id=5005&faqId=1817

Dobbs, D. (2012, December 7). The new temper tantrum disorder: Will the new diagnostic manual for psychiatrists go too far in labeling kids dysfunctional? *Slate*. Retrieved from http://www.slate.com/articles/double_x/doublex/2012/12/disruptive_mood_dysregulation_disorder_in_dsm_5_criticism_of_a_new_diagnosis.html

Eells, T. D. (Ed.). (2007). *Handbook of psychotherapy formulation* (2nd ed.). New York, NY: Guilford Press.

Eells, T. D., Lombart, K. G., Kendjelic, E. M., Turner, L. C., & Lucas, C. (2005). The quality of case formulations: A comparison of expert, experienced, and novice cognitive–behavioral and psychodynamic therapists. *Journal of Consulting and Clinical Psychology, 73,* 579–589. doi:10.1037/0022-006X.73.4.579

Egli, S., Schlatter, K., Streule, R., & Läge, D. (2006). A structure-based expert model of the ICD–10 mental disorders. *Psychopathology, 39,* 1–9. doi:10.1159/000089657

Evans, S. C., Reed, G. M., Correia, J. M., Ritchie, P., Watts, A. D., Esparza, P., . . . Saxena, S. (2013). Psychologists' perspectives on the diagnostic classification of mental disorders: Results from the WHO–IUPsyS Global Survey. *International Journal of Psychology, 48,* 177–193. doi:10.1080/00207594.2013.804189

First, M. B. (2010). Clinical utility in the revision of the Diagnostic and Statistical Manual of Mental Disorders (DSM). *Professional Psychology: Research and Practice, 41,* 465–473. doi:10.1037/a0021511

First, M. B., & Reed, G. M. (2013). *Working document: Analysis of ICD–10 Clinical Descriptions and Diagnostic Guidelines vs. ICD–10 CM (U.S.) differences.* Geneva, Switzerland: World Health Organization.

Flanagan, E. H., Keeley, J., & Blashfield, R. K. (2008). An alternative hierarchical organization of the mental disorders of *DSM–IV.*

Journal of Abnormal Psychology, 117, 693–698. doi:10.1037/a0012535

Forbes, D., Creamer, M., Bisson, J. I., Cohen, J. A., Crow, B. E., Foa, E. B., Friedman, M. J., . . . Ursano, R. J. (2010). A guide to guidelines for the treatment of PTSD and related conditions. *Journal of Traumatic Stress, 23,* 537–552. doi:10.1002/jts.20565

Garb, H. N. (2005). Clinical judgment and decision-making. *Annual Review of Clinical Psychology, 1,* 67–89. doi:10.1146/annurev.clinpsy.1.102803.143810

Giannangelo, K. (2011). *Transitioning to ICD–10–CM/PCS.* Chicago, IL: American Health Information Management Association.

Goodheart, C. D. (2006). *Evidence, endeavor, and expertise in psychology practice.* In C. D. Goodheart, A. E. Kazdin, & R. J. Sternberg (Eds.), *Evidence-based psychotherapy: Where practice and research meet* (pp. 37–62). Washington, DC: American Psychological Association.

Goodheart, C. D. (2011). Psychology practice: Design for tomorrow. *American Psychologist, 66,* 339–347. doi:10.1037/a0024222

Hansen, H. B., Donaldson, Z., Link, B. J., Bearman, P. S., Hopper, K., Bates, L. M., . . . Teitler, J. O. (2013). Independent review of social and population variation in mental health could improve diagnosis is DSM revisions. *Health Affairs, 32,* 984–993. doi:10.1377/hlthaff.2011.0596

Health Insurance Portability and Accountability Act of 1996, Pub. L. 104-191, 104 (1996).

Hersen, M., & Rosqvist, J. (2008). *Handbook of psychological assessment, case conceptualization and treatment: Vol. 1. Adults.* Hoboken, NJ: Wiley.

Horvath, A. O., & Bedi, R. P. (2002). The alliance. In J. C. Norcross (Ed.), *Psychotherapy relationships that work: Therapist contributions and responsiveness to patients.* New York, NY: Oxford University Press.

Hyman, S. E. (2010). The diagnosis of mental disorders: The problem of reification. *Annual Review of Clinical Psychology, 6,* 155–179. doi:10.1146/annurev.clinpsy.3.022806.091532

Ingram, B. L. (2003). Teaching case formulation skills to clinical graduate students. *PsycEXTRA Database Record*. Abstract retrieved from http://psycnet.apa.org/psycextra/340202004-001.pdf

Ingram, B. L. (2011). *Clinical case formulations: Matching the integrative treatment plan to the client* (2nd ed.). New York, NY: Wiley.

Insel, T. (2013, April 29). *Director's blog: Transforming diagnosis.* Retrieved from http://www.nimh.nih.gov/about/director/2013/transforming-diagnosis.shtml

International Statistical Institute. (1893). *International list of causes of death*. Paris, France: Author.

International Statistical Institute. (1900). *International list of causes of death* (1st rev.). Paris, France: Author.

International Statistical Institute. (1920). *International list of causes of death* (3rd rev.). Paris, France: Author.

Johnson, S. B. (2011, August). *ICD–11, DSM–5, and ICD–10–CM: APA's involvement and advocacy.* Paper presented at the annual convention of the American Psychological Association, Washington, DC.

Kendell, R., & Jablensky, A. (2003). Distinguishing between the validity and utility of psychiatric diagnoses. *The American Journal of Psychiatry, 160,* 4–12. doi:10.1176/appi.ajp.160.1.4

Kohn, R., Saxena, S., Levav, I., & Saraceno, B. (2004). Treatment gap in mental health care. *Bulletin of the World Health Organization, 82,* 858–866.

Kupfer, D. J., Kuhl, E. A., & Regier, D. A. (2013, February 25). DSM–5—The future arrived. *JAMA, 309*(16), 1691–1692. Retrieved from http://jama.jamanetwork.com/article.aspx?articleid=1656312

McWilliams, N. (1994). *Psychoanalytic diagnosis: Understanding personality structures in the clinical process.* New York, NY: Guilford Press.

Miller, S. D., Duncan, B. L., & Hubble, M. A. (2005). Outcome-informed clinical work. In J. C. Norcross & M. R. Goldfried (Eds.), *Handbook of psychotherapy integration* (2nd ed., pp. 84–102). New York, NY: Oxford University Press.

Mixed Commission. (1929). *International list of causes of death* (4th rev.). Paris, France: Author.

Mixed Commission. (1938). *International list of causes of death* (5th rev.). Paris, France: Author.

Moriyama, I. M., Loy, R. M., & Robb-Smith, A. H. T. (2011). *History of the statistical classification of diseases and causes of death.* Hyattsville, MD: National Center for Health Statistics. Retrieved from http://www.cdc.gov/nchs/data/misc/classification_diseases2011.pdf

Moynihan, R. (2011, May 3). A new deal on disease definition. *BMJ, 342,* d2548. doi:10.1136/bmj.d2548

National Center for Health Statistics and Centers for Medicare and Medicaid Services. (1979). *International Classification of Diseases, Clinical Modification.* Retrieved from http://www.cdc.gov/nchs/icd/icd9cm.htm

National Committee on Vital and Health Statistics. (2000). *50th Anniversary Symposium Reports.* Retrieved from http://www.cdc.gov/nchs/data/ncvhs/nchvs50th.pdf

PDM Task Force. (2006). *Psychodynamic diagnostic manual.* Silver Spring, MD: Alliance of Psychoanalytic Organizations.

Pickett, D. (2012). *Understanding the impact of the differences in ICD–9–CM and ICD–10–CM and its potential impact on data analysis.* Retrieved from http://www.cdc.gov/nchs/ppt/nchs2012/LI-01_PICKETT.pdf

Reed, G. M. (2010). Toward ICD–11: Improving the clinical utility of WHO's international classification of mental disorders. *Professional Psychology: Research and Practice, 41,* 457–464. doi:10.1037/a0021701

Reed, G. M. (2012, November). *The structure of the mental disorders chapter in ICD–11.* Paper presented at the meeting of the DGPPN Congress, Berlin, Germany.

Reed, G. M. (2013, August). *Global field studies of WHO's ICD–11: Preliminary results.* Paper presented at the meeting of the American Psychological Association, Honolulu, HI.

Reed, G. M., Correia, J. M., Esparza, P., Saxena, S., & Maj, M. (2011). The WPA–WHO global survey of psychiatrists' attitudes towards mental disorders classification. *World Psychiatry, 10,* 118–131.

Reed, G. M., Dua, T., & Saxena, S. (2011, May 11). Who should define disease? *BMJ, 342,* d2974. doi:10.1136/bmj.d2974

Reed, G. M., Roberts, M. C., Keeley, J. W., Hooppell, C., Matsumoto, C., Sharan, P., . . . Medina-Mora, M. E. (2013). Mental health professionals' natural taxonomies of mental disorders: Implications for the clinical utility of the ICD–11 and the DSM–5. *Journal of Clinical Psychology.* Advanced online publication. doi:10.1002/jclp.22031

Ritchie, P. L.-J. (2013). *World Health Organization (WHO) ICD–10 revision.* Retrieved from http://www.apa.org/international/outreach/who-icd-revision.aspx

Roberts, M. C., & Evans, S. C. (2013). Using the International Classification of Diseases (ICD–10). In G. Koocher, J. Norcross, & B. Greene (Eds.), *The psychologist's desk reference* (3rd ed., pp. 71–76). New York, NY: Oxford University Press.

Roberts, M. C., Reed, G. M., Medina-Mora, M. E., Keeley, J. W., Sharon, P., Johnson, D. K., . . . Saxena, S. (2012). A global clinicians map of mental disorders to improve ICD–11: Analysing meta-structure to enhance clinical utility. *International Review of Psychiatry, 24,* 578–590. doi:10.3109/09540261.2012.736368

Sturmey, P. (2008). *Behavioral Case Formulation.* Chichester, England: Wiley. doi:10.1002/9780470773192

Sturmey, P. (Ed.). (2009). *Case formulation: Varieties of approaches.* Chichester, England: Wiley–Blackwell. Retrieved from http://toniau.ac.ir/doc/books/Clinical%20Case%20Formulation.pdf

Taylor, S. E., Klein, L. C., Lewis, B. P., Gruenewald, T. L., Gurung, R. A. R., & Updegraff, J. A. (2000). Biobehavioral responses to stress in females: Tend-and-befriend, not fight-or-flight. *Psychological Review, 107,* 411–429. doi:10.1037/0033-295X.107.3.411

U.S. Department of Commerce and Labor. (1909). *International classification of causes of sickness and death.* Washington, DC: Government Printing Office.

Viera, A. J., & Garrett, J. M. (2005). Understanding interobserver agreement: The kappa statistic. *Family Medicine, 37,* 360–363. Retrieved from http://www1.cs.columbia.edu/~julia/courses/CS6998/Interrater_agreement.Kappa_statistic.pdf

Vijayan, S. (2007). A World Health Organization primer. *MedGenMed: Medscape General Medicine, 9*(4), 41–46. Retrieved from http://www.ncbi.nlm.nih.gov/pmc/articles/PMC2234304/

Wiser, S., & Goldfried, M. R. (1998). Therapist interventions and client emotional experiencing in expert psychodynamic–interpersonal and cognitive–behavioral therapies. *Journal of Consulting and Clinical Psychology, 66,* 634–640. doi:10.1037/0022-006X.66.4.634

World Health Organization. (1948). *International classification of diseases and related health problems* (6th rev.). Geneva, Switzerland: Author.

World Health Organization. (1955). *International classification of diseases and related health problems* (7th rev.). Geneva, Switzerland: Author.

World Health Organization. (1965). *International classification of diseases and related health problems* (8th rev.). Geneva, Switzerland: Author.

World Health Organization. (1979). *International classification of diseases and related health problems* (9th rev.). Geneva, Switzerland: Author.

World Health Organization. (1992a). *International classification of diseases and related health problems* (10th rev.). Geneva, Switzerland: Author.

World Health Organization. (1992b). ICD–10 *Classification of mental and behavioural disorders: Clinical descriptions and diagnostic guidelines.* Retrieved from http://www.who.int/classifications/icd/en/bluebook.pdf

World Health Organization. (1993). *The ICD–10 classification of mental and behavioural disorders: Diagnostic criteria for research.* Retrieved from http://www.who.int/classifications/icd/en/GRNBOOK.pdf

World Health Organization. (1996). *Diagnostic and management guidelines for mental disorders in primary care: ICD–10 Chapter V primary care version.* WHO/Hogrefe & Huber Publishers. Gottingen, Germany.

World Health Organization. (2001). *The international classification of functioning, disability, and health* (ICF). Retrieved from http://www.who.int/classifications/icf/en/

World Health Organization. (2008). *The global burden of disease: 2004 update.* Geneva, Switzerland: Author.

World Health Organization. (2010). *ICD-10: Version 2010.* Geneva, Switzerland: Author. Retrieved from http://apps.who.int/classifications/icd10/browse/2010/en#/V

World Health Organization. (2013a). *About WHO.* Retrieved from http://www.who.int/about/structure/en/

World Health Organization. (2013b). *International Classification of Diseases* (ICD). Retrieved from http://www.who.int/classifications/icd/en/

World Health Organization. (2013c). *WHO Disability Assessment Schedule 2.0 WHODAS 2.0.* Retrieved from http://www.who.int/classifications/icf/whodasii/en/

World Health Organization. (n.d.). *History of the development of the ICD.* Retrieved from http://www.who.int/classifications/icd/en/HistoryOfICD.pdf

World Health Organization World Mental Health Survey Consortium. (2004). Prevalence, severity, and unmet need for treatment of mental disorders in the World Health Organization World Mental Health surveys. *Journal of the American Medical Association, 291,* 2581–2590. doi:10.1001/jama.291.21.2581

Zeisset, A. M., & Bowman, S. E. (2010). *Pocket Guide of ICD–10–CM and ICD–10–PCS.* Chicago, IL: American Health Information Management Association.

Index

About the Author

Carol D. Goodheart, EdD, is in independent practice in Princeton, New Jersey, and is past president of the American Psychological Association. Her career integrates practice, scholarship, and service to psychology. Dr. Goodheart works at the intersection of physical and mental health, practice and science, humanism and scholarship. Before becoming a psychologist, Dr. Goodheart trained as a nurse. She worked in urban emergency medicine and intensive care, as well as rural public health on two Native American reservations. She earned her doctorate in counseling psychology from Rutgers University, and she specializes in the treatment of individuals, couples, and families coping with physical diseases or disabilities

In addition to her practice, she has served at Rutgers University's Graduate School of Applied and Professional Psychology in a number of roles: clinical supervisor, contributing faculty, and committee on continuing education. She is a founding partner of two organizations: PsychHealth, PA, a multi-specialty mental health practice offering treatment services, program design, and consultation, primarily in health psychology; and W2W, LLC, dedicated to the development and dissemination of materials designed to build strengths, promote health, and enhance quality of life for women.